Discipleship *Un*complicated

The 8 Principles of Disciple Making

DR. WARREN HAYNES

Carpenter's Son Publishing

*This book is dedicated
to my wife Janice and our children:
Ivory, Chloe, Auburn, and Asher.
You are the best!*

Contents

Acknowledgments

Many people have loved me and pointed me to Jesus. For some our paths crossed for but a moment, but the mark they left was permanent. For others we have walked together for years, and their influence has been a slow and steady stream of spiritual direction and encouragement. Every moment and every encounter has served to challenge, inspire, and propel me to keep walking with Jesus, I thank God for you. Connie Roberts, Justin Haynes, John Heath, and James Vaughn had special roles to play in my life. In her 70s Connie took it upon herself to introduce me to Jesus. Justin has been the best brother I could hope for; he has given unconditionally, prayed unceasingly, and has encouraged me to give my best to Jesus. While I was in college, John Heath made it his responsibility to teach me how to listen and respond to God in everyday life. James invited me to live with him and his family to show me what it looks and feels like to minister God's love to others. I thank God for you. To anyone who would dare to pick up a book about disciple making, you are amazing and I thank God for you. All the good that is in this book and comes from this book is owed to Jesus.

Introduction

In *Discipleship Uncomplicated* I promise to share with you in understandable terms what you have to do to make disciples. Each principle has five sections that seamlessly integrate disciple making into everyday life.

First, each principle begins with a biblical foundation. In preparation for this work, I looked at every occasion in the Bible where Jesus encountered another person, and I asked two foundational questions: (1) What did Jesus literally say? and (2) What did Jesus actually do? So what you are introduced to in *Discipleship Uncomplicated* is birthed from the Bible and practiced by Jesus.

Second, for each principle, I share inspiring real-life stories that are encouraging, fun, challenging, and insightful.

Third, each principle has a "How It Works and Why It Matters" section. In this section I reveal how and why each disciple-making practice works.

Fourth, there is a section called "The Practical" that takes the guesswork out of the discipleship process and spells out exactly how you can begin making disciples.

Lastly, after I explain each principle, there is a challenge for you to complete.

It takes action to make disciples. Therefore, the goal of *Discipleship Uncomplicated* is not information retention, but rather to help you integrate actions into your daily life that empower you to experience real-life disciple making. In the gospel of Matthew, Jesus teaches a tale of two men: a wise man and a foolish man. Both of these men knew what God was asking them to do but only one of them took action. Action reveals wisdom! Disciple-making success boils down to your willingness to take action in the moments the Holy Spirit gives you direction.

Discipleship Uncomplicated introduces you to the engine that powers disciple making. When you spot a good-looking car or truck, your eyes are drawn to the striking colors, the sleek lines, or the vehicle's looks. However, it is the engine that powers the vehicle. The engine often goes unnoticed. As you turn the pages of *Discipleship Uncomplicated*, I am going to lift the hood and show you the cylinders that provide the horsepower for disciple making.

These skills often go unnoticed, but I guarantee you that people who are successful at disciple making practice what I am going to share with you. These skills that you are about to discover were practiced by Jesus, and they will empower you to become a disciple maker.

If you keep your heart bent on loving God and loving people while putting in the effort to discover, develop, and propel these disciple-making skills into action, you will become a disciple who makes disciples. May the LORD Jesus Christ bless your work, may He fill you with joy, and may many people come to know, love, and follow Him.

Now it's time to tune your engine.

Principle 1

Love God, Love People

The Heartbeat of Disciple Making

B efore jumping into what it takes to make disciples, let's define the concept of disciple making. Disciples of Jesus are those who deny themselves, take up their cross, and follow Him every day—and someone who empowers others to do the same. Jesus said if someone were going to follow Him, that is what they would need to do (Luke 9:23). He also charged his disciples to make disciples (Matthew 28:18-20). Simply put, a disciple is someone who follows Jesus and influences others to follow Him. A disciple is a person who emulates His life, wears His words, and embodies His mission. Having defined what a disciple is, there are a few things to keep in mind as we embark on this disciple-making journey together.

First, this journey to disciple making starts with heart. The heart of disciple making is loving God and loving people. Love gives meaning, purpose, fuel, and fulfillment to disciple making.

As the Gospels pour out the life of Jesus, we are refreshed by a life that gushes with an irrefutable love. This love fuels every step, overcomes every challenge, gives laughter to every joy, and covers every wrong. Disciple making is powerless without love. It takes love to make a disciple, and this love flows from your heart. Above everything else guard your own heart, Proverbs 4:23 tells us. It is the spring from which your life flows.

A friend of mine has a saying which goes, "In real estate it's location, location, location. In ministry it's relationship, relationship, relationship." Love God, love people. These phrases capture the most important relationships in life. They express the supreme purposes for living. They fulfill the greatest commandments God has given us. They are what every word in the Bible is moving us to do. I have come to realize that there is no way I can ever overstate their significance.

For me this has been a profound discovery of the obvious. It has always been there in plain sight. I have literally read it hundreds of times. I have committed it to memory. I have used it while speaking to crowds and individuals. This discovery has certainly caused me to wonder how could I look at something so often and not really see it. Believe me, it happens—it happens to all of us.

Early one morning during our first year of marriage, my wife, Janice, looked at me and said, "Blink your eyes." I thought maybe she wanted me to wink at her, so I obliged. She said, "Do it again." So I blinked my eyes like crazy and she began to laugh. I asked, "What's going on? What is so funny?" to which she replied, "Did you know that when you blink your eyes a little place on your nose moves?"

2

"Are you serious?"

"Yes, go look in the mirror and blink one eye and see if you can see it."

Low and behold, it was true. I could see it clear as crystal. For the first time in twenty-five-plus years, I saw something that was literally as plain as the nose on my face. Every time I blink my eyes my nose moves. She calls it a "nose blink" and claims it is proof that my wires are crossed.

Well, for the first time after years of looking at a familiar passage, I discovered something that has brought clarity to how I think about the Bible and purpose to how I live my life. Here is the passage where I discovered it. Take a moment, read over this passage carefully, and see if you can see it.

Hearing that Jesus had silenced the Sadducees, the Pharisees got together. One of them, an expert in the law, tested him with this question: "Teacher, which is the greatest commandment in the Law?" Jesus replied: 'Love the Lord your God with all your heart and with all your soul and with all your mind.' This is the first and greatest commandment. And the second is like it: 'Love your neighbor as yourself.' All the Law and the Prophets hang on these two commandments." (Matthew 22:34-40)

Did you catch it? OK, maybe that is a little vague. You are about to discover a profound truth that will illuminate how you read the Bible and how you relate to God and people every day once it grips you. Use the passage above to answer the following questions.

Quick Quiz

1. The Pharisee who tested Jesus was an expert in the _____. (It's like being an expert in the Bible.)
2. What is the first and greatest commandment? _____ God.
3. What is the second greatest commandment? _____ people.
4. How much of the Bible hangs on these two commandments? _____

(Answers: 1. Law 2. Love 3. Love 4. All)

Did you catch it? The truth I'm referring to is captured in the fourth question above. How much of the Bible depends on loving God and loving people? _____ of it. In a brief response Jesus brought all the complexity of the Bible into vivid clarity.

The entire Bible—every word, every phrase, every thought, every passage, every poem, every song, every story, every person, and every prophecy—depends completely on two commandments. Love God! Love people! If the entire Bible depends on these two commandments, then the entire Bible leads us to live these two commandments. Every word of the Bible is leading us to love God and love people. If we miss this, we miss everything. Loving God and loving people is the beating heart of disciple making.

Next, it takes laser focus on two key outcomes to walk in the footprints of Jesus: developing leaders and reaching new people. Jesus was always developing a few and reaching the new. These two pursuits form the unbreakable bones of disciple making. In disciple making there is a constant motion of learning and sharing that transpires, like the constant motion of the waves on a seashore. Developing leaders and reaching new people are the constant motion of disciple making. It takes focus on developing those who will follow you and always reaching out to the new people around you. It is vital to keep one eye on developing others and one eye on reaching others. Jesus developed the Twelve and reached new people in the crowds.

Read the following passage (the Great Commission) and answer the question:

Therefore go and make disciples of people from all nations, baptizing them in the name of the Father, in the name of the Son, and in the name of the Holy Spirit. Teach them and show them how to live the commands I have given to you. And I will always be with you. (author's paraphrase of Matthew 28:18-20)

Quick Quiz

Which one of the following did Jesus ask His followers to do?

_____1. Be a disciple.

_____2. Make disciples.

_____3. Train your dog.

If you opened door number two, then you are the grand prize winner. Jesus said, "Go and make disciples." This is clear. So what is the fundamental difference between being a disciple and making a disciple? And why bother asking the question? I believe for decades we have focused on being disciples and, as a result, we have drifted from what Jesus has asked us to do.

Here is the difference between focusing on being a disciple and focusing on making disciples and why it matters. I can be a disciple all by myself, but I can't make a disciple by myself. Disciple making requires another human being. If we focus on being a disciple instead of making disciples then, left unchecked, we begin to drift toward self-improvement as the goal.

We begin to pray, read the Bible, attend worship, and do good so we will feel better about ourselves. And how we feel about ourselves then become our unsatisfying purpose for living. If we are not careful, we can live our entire lives in the pursuit of self-fulfillment cloaked in spiritual jargon and meaningless motion.

Loving God and loving people is the pursuit of pleasing God and empowering others. On a foundational level, disciple making requires that we focus on inspiring others to love and follow Jesus. Being a disciple focuses on me. Making a disciple focuses on another. Growing churches and organizations do two things well. They develop leaders and they reach new people. Disciple making requires focus on someone other than ourselves.

Third, is takes learnable skills to make disciples. Disciple making is not a spiritual gift reserved for only a few elite super Christians. Disciple making is the primary mandate that Jesus gave to every person who would deny himself, take up his cross, and follow Him. Disciple making is not sitting in a class collecting biblical knowledge. It is growing your awareness and developing skills that empower you to take action to help people get on the path to following Jesus.

It's not about having a particular personality, disposition, or giftedness. Rather, it's about applying discipline and getting the guidance you need to be successful. Every world-champion athlete has to develop their skills. They start like everybody else: learning to crawl, learning to walk, then learning to run. They develop their muscles and hone their skills by putting in the necessary work and seeking out expert guidance.

I once listened to billionaire Paul Mitchell, who founded Paul Mitchell Salons and has world-recognized hair and beauty product lines, share some of his life lessons. He shared an experience from a time in his life when he worked for a dry cleaner, making twenty-five cents an hour. Here is the life lesson Paul shared: "Successful people do what unsuccessful people are not willing to do." This is true in churches, ministries, and personal impact. Successful disciple makers are willing to do what unsuccessful disciple makers are not willing to do.

It takes discipline and expert guidance to become excellent at anything. This is true for making disciples. I can show you the skills to practice, but you have to put in the reps for you to see personal results. If you put in the work, God will give the results.

In this technological age of disconnected screen zombies, discovering and developing disciple-making skills is a must if we are going to fulfill the mission that Jesus gave us to accomplish. A skill is something you can learn, something you can practice, something you can improve. That means you can do this! Disciple-making skills are the muscles that move disciple making into everyday life.

So start with a heart that beats with loving God and loving people. Focus on developing those who you can influence and reaching out to new people. Apply yourself to the daily practice of developing disciple-making skills. It takes love, focus, and skills to make disciples.

Now that we have covered the basic foundation for disciple making, it's time to spell out exactly what a person has to do to make disciples, and it's NOT complicated.

Principle 2

What's Your Name?

Make Disciple Making Personal

T he most important word in any language is someone's **name**. A person's name is significant because it is tied to one's life, potential, and purpose. A person's name can immediately move a conversation or encounter from the general to the specific, from everyone's opportunity to my opportunity. If you want to get someone's attention, call his name.

Notice that God called people by name when He wanted to involve them in His work. When God wanted to get the attention of Moses, He called him by name. "God called to him from within the burning bush, 'Moses! Moses!'" (Exodus 3:4).

When He wanted to get Samuel started, He called him by Name. "The LORD came and stood there, calling as at the other times, 'Samuel! Samuel!'" (1 Samuel 3:10).

When Jesus wanted to enter the world of a vertically challenged tax collector, He called him by name his name, Zacchaeus (Luke 19:5).

When the LORD wanted to turn Saul's life around, He called him by name. "[Saul] fell to the ground and heard a voice say to him, 'Saul, Saul, . . .'" (Acts 9:4).

Today the Good Shepherd "calls his own sheep by name and leads them out" (John 10:3).

When God wanted His people to know they were not forgotten, He said, "I will not forget you. See, I have written your name on the palms of my hands" (Isaiah 49:15-16 NLT).

God calls us by name so our names will make the most important list: those "whose names are in the book of life" (Philippians 4:3).

We are following God's lead when we learn and use a person's name.

Discipleship Uncomplicated begins when we care enough to get to know someone's name. Take a moment and consider that the God of the universe who put the stars in place, who determined the boundaries of the seas, who created gravity and every living thing not only knows your name—He calls you by name. Your name is important and so is the name of your neighbor.

Once, a friend and I were going through a neighborhood trying to find people we could help. I find that this exercise sharpens my awareness and keeps me in touch with the real world.

In the first house we came to we found a young woman and man outside smoking cigarettes. After a little chitchat we discovered that this young woman (we will call her Tonya) was a new mother. She recently gave birth to a baby girl who came into this world with some health issues. We learned that Tonya was not married, and neither she nor her boyfriend had a job. We learned that Tonya's father was not happy with the arrangement and didn't want them living in his house. Let's just say in a matter of moments we learned way more than we bargained for. We asked them both what they thought about Jesus and there was clearly NO interest. It seemed with every question we asked, the deeper the rabbit hole went and the darker the situation became. But, let's be real: this is where many people live every day. We asked Tonya what she needed for her baby girl. She said with obvious concern, "Everything! We have nothing and we really don't know how things are going to turn out. She is still very sick." We let her know that we would do something to help. I didn't know exactly what that would be at the time, but I knew we could do something. We can always do something.

Before we left we asked if we could pray for them, and they agreed that prayer would be helpful. There is something about prayer that is good. Prayer connects us with something greater than ourselves. Prayer brings hope. After we said our prayers and good-byes, we sent out an email to some ladies in the church explaining Tonya's need.

This was about noon on Saturday; by Sunday morning the ladies had filled sacks with baby supplies and had prepared a special gift for Tonya. It was one of those moments that truly made me proud to be a part of such a great group—the church! This is what it means to be salt and light so people can taste and see that the Lord is good.

After we left Tonya's house, we had an encounter three doors down. We were welcomed in from the cold, for which I was very appreciative. The saying in Northwest Indiana is there are two seasons: winter and construction. All I can tell you is there is a legitimate reason for this saying!

I could tell right away that this man was a strict religious dude! We will call him Ebenezer. I chose this name for a specific reason that I will reveal at the end of this story.

After interacting with many people, I have developed a feel for such encounters, and I was right. Ebenezer was courteous, to the extent that he invited us in from the cold. Then he began his line of questioning with something like "Hello, what are you guys doing?"

"We are out looking for people to help."

"What version of the Bible do you use?"

This conversation was beginning to feel like the skier on ABC's *Wide World of Sports* or a skateboarder on a YouTube video. The agony of defeat, the hardcore crash, or a spot on *America's Funniest Home Videos* was forming quickly. How do you go from "Hey, how are you guys doing?" to "I don't like you if you don't read the *right* version of the Bible?"

Undeterred, I pressed on. "I read multiple versions of the Bible, and if I am looking for clarity, I will explore the biblical text in the Hebrew or Greek." I knew this would impress Ebenezer, or at least it would reveal to him that I gave an honest effort to my study of the biblical text.

Ebenezer was not impressed, however! He said something to the effect of "If you don't use the King James version of the Bible, you are living in darkness."

"I value the King James," I said. "It has helped many people have a better relationship with God. I still have and cherish the King James Bible my brother gave me when I was a teenager."

"You just don't get it," he countered. "You will never come to the truth if you don't read the King James."

Yikes, what had I gotten us into? I could tell by the look on the face of the young man who was with me that he was thinking something similar to *I'm never going anywhere with this guy ever again!*

After a mini lecture on the supremacy of the King James, Ebenezer was ready to crawl up onto his next soap box: worship. It was at this moment that Ebenezer's wife walked into the room and sat beside her husband. She was petite and proper and she had a pleasant look on her face. I quickly surmised that this woman will get many rewards in heaven for what she has likely endured on Earth.

But back to the worship soapbox. "So when you sing do you sing off the wall or from a hymnal?" Ebenezer asked.

At this point I thought, *Well, if you are standing next to me while I am singing, you would probably think that I sing off the wall.* But I said, "Well, Jesus said that true worshipers, the kind God is looking for, worship Him in the Spirit and in truth" (referring to John 4:23-24).

I continued, "To worship in spirit means you are present in the moment. That Jesus has your mind's attention and your heart's affection. To worship in truth means authenticity. If someone were standing next to me as I worshiped, would he believe that I believe what I am singing? Would my singing inspire him to sing to God?"

Ebenezer responded with something tantamount to "Well, if you don't sing from the hymnal, then you probably don't love Jesus." That might be an overstatement, but it heads toward the intended target.

13

This was the moment where everything changed. An intriguing question had come to mind and I wanted to know the answer. "Ebenezer, would you mind if I asked you a question?"

Being polite, he agreed.

"Do you know your neighbor who lives three doors down from you?" I pointed toward the direction of Tonya's house. "Do you know her name?"

"No!" Ebenezer said. "I have no idea."

"Let me tell you about your neighbor Tonya. She just had a baby girl who has been in the hospital. She is very worried about her daughter's health. She is young and unmarried. Neither she nor her boyfriend have a job. Her dad doesn't like being stuck with her and her sick baby at the house, and she has hardly any supplies to care for her daughter. Ebenezer, can you tell me how much Tonya is going to care about what version of the Bible you read or whether you sing projected words or written ones?"

The blank expression on his face spoke volumes about how far we all can drift when we are caught in the undertow of spiritual activity apart from real love for those around us. In a surreal moment, I watched as his wife shook her head up and down, profusely affirming the truth that we all know in our hearts. Our love for God is tied to our love for people and our love for people is tied to our love for God. How much can we love our neighbor if we don't even know her name?

So why did I choose to name this man "Ebenezer" for this story? It wasn't because he reminded me of Ebenezer Scrooge from *A Christmas Carol*, though correlations could be drawn. No, it was because in the Bible an "Ebenezer" was a stone that had been set in place like a marker so people would remember God's leadership (it's mentioned in 1 Kings 7:12). This encounter has become a stone of remembrance for me. This is what I look like to my neighbors when I live by them for years and don't even know their names. Therefore, I have determined that if I am going to love people, then I need to care enough to know their names, starting with my neighbors.

I asked a good friend of mine how many neighbors he knew by name. He responded maybe six or seven. I asked him how long he had lived in his house. He said, "Twenty-nine years." I challenged him to get to know people in his neighborhood by name and begin to pray with them and for them.

About four weeks later we ran into each other and I could tell he was excited. I asked him how many of his neighbors he knew by name and he responded, "Forty!" We celebrated as he told me how God was working through his prayers and how door after door had opened for him to get to know and encourage the people he had lived next to for so long.

What a difference being intentional can make. Six or seven people in twenty-nine years or forty people in four weeks? Getting to know people takes being intentional. Make a point of learning people's names, writing them down, and praying for them. It can make a profound difference in your life and theirs.

I have a friend named Bill who has been a pastor for years. He loves his family, has led many to Jesus, and has invested his life in honoring God and helping people. Recently Bill shared with me how he began this journey so many years ago.

As a young man he was a hippy who loved to smoke weed. One day he was invited to come to church, and even though it wasn't his scene, he decided to go. Bill described the man who greeted him that morning as a short, bald, round redneck who shook his hand and invited him in. Bill didn't remember too much about his first experience, but he decided to go back about three weeks later. As he entered the door, the short, bald, round redneck called his name, saying "Bill, it's so good to see you again." Bill was shocked that anyone would remember him at all, much less remember his name.

Bill told me it was that expression of love (remembering his name) that made the difference in his coming back and ultimately his coming to faith in Jesus Christ. If you were to ask Bill what difference remembering someone's name makes, he would tell you it has made a major difference in his family, his direction in life, and his relationship with God.

How It Works and Why It Matters

Asking another person "What's your name?" is the beginning of real-world disciple making. In the Bible, every time God the Father, the Son, or the Holy Spirit called someone by name, He changed their life. We rarely think that something as mundane as calling someone by name can become the epicenter for life change, but often that is exactly the case.

Getting to know someone by name is the first thing we can do to foundationally change our relationship with them. When we encounter any new group of people, we are part of the "everybody." When we get to know and call people by name and they call us by name, we become "somebody." A person's name is powerful because it is tied to their personhood. That's why if you are in a crowd and someone calls your name, you look. They are not just calling a name; they are calling you. That is also why it is NEVER a good idea to say, "I have forgotten your name," because, in essence, you are saying, "I have forgotten *you*."

How important is getting to know someone by name to disciple making? It is impossible to disciple someone you don't know and can't contact. That sounds like a no-brainer until you ask the second question. How many people who claim Christ and fill pews do you know who have an active growing list of names and best contact information of people they are actively striving to influence for Jesus? There is a massive gap between what we know makes since and what we actually practice.

What would you *pay* for a list of names and contact information of the people your organization is *guaranteed* most likely to influence for Christ?

You can't buy a list like this, but you can build one. By creating a Reach List, a person or group can begin to identify the people they are most likely to influence for Christ based on two principles: proximity and purpose.

Principle #1: Proximity

We are most likely to influence the people we are closest to. (Eight out of ten people come into a relationship with Jesus or the church through the influence of a friend, family member, coworker, or acquaintance.) This is the power of proximity.

Principle #2: Purpose

We are most likely to influence the people we are purposely trying to influence. Therefore, based on the principles of Proximity and

Purpose, a person or group can build a list of names and contact information that clearly identifies the people they are most likely to influence for Christ.

Exchanging names is the first move we can make to apply the principle of Proximity. This one skill quickly moves us from everyone to someone from the general to the personal. Meeting people and exchanging names and contact information is a skill we must develop if we are going to make disciples. Because let's face it, it is impossible to disciple someone we don't know and can't contact. As we develop this skill, we find that meeting new people is not only essential for disciple making—it is also a lot of fun.

It's Time to Get Started!

To get started I am going to help you make a Reach List with people's names and their best contact information. A Reach List is a list of people you know personally (or you want to get acquainted with) along with their best contact information. These are the people you will intentionally begin to disciple as followers of Jesus Christ. The first action you can take to make a disciple is to get to know someone's name and how to contact them. Here's is how you can get started today.

The Practical: How to Make a Reach List

Who goes on the list? People you know or meet who need to follow Jesus.

TIP #1 Think about your family and relatives who are currently not following Jesus, or those who you don't know where they are with Jesus. Think through fathers, mothers, sisters, brothers, cousins, nephews, nieces, aunts, uncles, grandparents, and extended family. Write the names that come to mind on the list provided later on. You can go back and add their contact information later.

TIP #2 Write the names of friends, coworkers, acquaintances, and neighbors who need to follow Jesus, or those who you're not sure where they are with Jesus. It is important to note that most people who come to a life-changing relationship with Jesus Christ do so because of the encouragement of a family member or friend.

TIP #3 If you have a list of contacts on your phone, scroll through them and write down those who need to follow Jesus or those who you're not sure where they are with Jesus and put them on your Reach List. You can do the same thing with Facebook and other forms of social media.

TIP #4 The important thing is not how many people you have on your list, but that you are beginning to take spiritual responsibility for others by putting them on your Reach List. **Always keep adding to your list.**

TIP #5 A good disciple maker exchanges names with people he meets. This week make a goal to exchange names with at least one person and put them on your Reach List. Give your name before you request theirs. Just one person a week will add fifty-two persons a year to your Reach List.

TIP #6 As soon as you meet a person, write his/her name and where you met him/her. Carry a small pad and pen if you prefer going old school or use your smartphone if tech is your style. It doesn't matter what you use as long as you get to know people by name. If you meet them where they work and cannot get their contact info, put down the place you met them in the best contact area.

TIP #7 If you have met someone before, but you can't remember their name, here is what you do. Smile, make brief eye contact, and say, "I remember you. Could you remind me of your name?" Then write it down. Using their name during the conversation is also very helpful. When asking for a name, keep a pleasant tone of voice.

TIP #8 As soon as you can, start praying for the people you meet by name. Prayer is essential for making disciples and very helpful for remembering people by name. You will find as you pray for people by name, you don't forget their name and God begins to increase your love and compassion for them.

TIP #9 Share how to make a Reach List with one person this week. Making disciples requires sharing what we learn with others. If we are not teaching others, we are not making disciples. Keep your list with you or where it's visible.

TIP #10 Read the next principle, "Let's Pray." Getting to know people's names and being able to contact them is the first step in the disciple making. The next step is learning how pray for them.

Challenge

Make a Reach List with a minimum of five names, then teach one other person how to create a list like yours.

My Reach List

Name	Best Contact

Discipleship Uncomplicated

Name	Best Contact

Principle 3

Let's Pray

Bring Spiritual Power to Your Relationships

Getting to know someone by name makes it personal. Praying for them makes it spiritually powerful! Prayer unlocks disciple making. Prayer is powerful and is absolutely paramount in the disciple-making process. We find in the book of James that the prayer of a person believing God is powerful and productive (James 5:16). This means the prayers you and I pray for those we are working with are also powerful and productive.

What makes prayer powerful? Is it using long words? Or trying to impress people with biblical knowledge? Is it knowing the right things to say?

NO!

God's presence is what makes prayers powerful. The Bible reveals that "the Lord our God is near us" whenever we pray to Him (Deuteronomy 4:7). So whenever we pray with other people, a powerful encounter with God is possible.

At a certain point in his ministry, Jesus spent the night in prayer, asking God for wisdom in selecting the Twelve. The next morning, he "called his disciples" to him and "chose twelve of them" (Luke 6:13). Disciple making is a spiritual endeavor, and praying for those we will influence is of primary importance. We need to be asking God to reveal to us those we can begin to disciple. As God reveals people we can influence, we need to put them on our Reach List. Our Reach List then becomes our disciple-making PRAYER LIST.

Jesus prayed specifically for and with His disciples. When Jesus was praying in John 17, His disciples were with Him, and He prayed specifically for them. In this chapter of the Bible, we get to peer through the windowpane and watch and listen in on just one of the many times Jesus prayed with His disciples. Let's eavesdrop on this powerful prayer time with His followers.

About His disciples, He said, "I pray for them. I am not praying for the world, but for those you have given me" (John 17:9). If the disciples had not been present, this prayer would not have been recorded! It took a few readings for the reality of their presence to sink in. Jesus didn't just go out and pray by Himself; He also prayed with His disciples. Here Jesus is specifically praying for and with them. In this stunning verse Jesus is not praying for everybody, but only for His disciples. Here his focus was not on the world, but on those who would change the world.

In that prayer Jesus prayed specific things for His disciples. He prayed that the Father would protect them (John 17:11). He prayed with them so they could experience God's full measure of joy (v. 13). He prayed that God would protect them from the evil one (v. 15). He prayed that God would set them apart for His sacred work through an undeterred reliance on God's Word (vv. 17-18). Specific prayers are powerful prayers.

The disciples heard Jesus express His desires for them in this prayer. They listened as He voiced to God His yearning that they would be with Him, and that they would personally know God the Father and share fully in their relationship (vv. 24-25). The disciples heard Jesus praying that the love of God would be in them just like the love of God was in Jesus Himself (v. 26). How could those present not be encouraged after personally hearing Jesus pray over them in this manner?

I can't help but think if you and I could have been there and heard with our own ears Jesus praying for us in this manner, it would have fashioned an unforgettable, emboldening experience. Don't you?

Then let these words that Jesus prayed during that prayer speak directly to you. "My prayer is not for them alone. I pray also for those who will believe in me through their message" (John 17:20). Jesus did pray for you, me, and those we will disciple during that prayer. He prayed personally and specifically that we would believe, that we would come together as one, and that the world would believe and experience His love through us (vv. 20-23).

The baseline practice of Jesus in this setting should fuel the fires of prayer for those in our lives. If Jesus prayed for and with His disciples, we should pray for and with those we are making into disciples. We are following Jesus' example when we pray specifically with the people on our Reach List. It's easier to disciple someone if we are praying specifically for and with him or her.

Jesus told His disciples that there are some things going on in people's lives that can only be resolved through focused, concentrated praying (Mark 9:29). As followers of Jesus we face a very complex world filled with labels that raise blinding blockades and accentuate differences that expand the distance between us and the people we are striving to influence for Christ.

We face unseen spiritual forces that mar human decency, corrupt common courtesies, and cripple compassion (Ephesians 6:12). That is why prayer is so important. Prayer connects us to God and God blows up the biggest barriers, closes the farthest distances, and annihilates evil forces. Prayer changes everything!

Praying with a person is often an unforgettable gift that few people outside the walls of the church actually experience. Praying with a person connects us to God's love for them, and it helps them connect to His love. Once, a friend and I were out in a community praying with people. The first person we met was a man named Rico. He had a little girl wrapped around his leg as he stood in the doorway. During the conversation we discovered that Rico was in need of work.

As a father I connected with Rico's desire to provide for his family and genuinely wanted to be a help and an encouragement to him. We prayed with Rico that God would protect, watch over, and provide him with work so he could take care of his family. We prayed that Rico would experience the power of God in his life and would know Jesus personally, and other good things that came to mind. After we said amen, he shook our hands enthusiastically and thanked us for the prayers. We were all very encouraged.

We went a couple houses down, and there stood a very large man who appeared to blot out the sun. He looked like a professional wrestler who might have "The Mauler" as part of his moniker. He had just put his wife and child in the car and waited as we approached. As we closed the distance, I introduced myself and my friend by first names and asked him for his name. He said in a pounding bass voice, "My name is Mohammed." I noticed his necklace bearing the crescent moon and star and surmised that Mohammed, by name and accessories, was a practicing Muslim.

In a deep rumbling voice that made me question my manhood, he asked, "What are you guys doing?"

"We are out in the community praying with people," I replied. "We know God loves people and He loves you and we want to pray for you and your family. Would that be all right?"

He said, "Sure."

My experience in interactions with people has taught me that most of what I fear in these types of encounters is not real, so proceed. To appreciate this encounter, you need to visualize three grown men from very different upbringings. There we were: Mohammed, a mountain of a Muslim man; my short, round friend who pastored a nearby church; and me. Physically different, religiously different, socially different, economically different, racially different, and educationally different—all standing in Mohammed's front yard, holding hands like school kids, praying together. The mental image still brings a chuckle and a smile.

After we prayed for Mohammed and his family, everyone said amen. And I was totally unprepared for what happened next. Mohammed grabbed me by the arms with his massive meat hooks. I envisioned a devastating signature wrestling move was coming and there was no hope of escape. Instead, he said in a nerve-rattling voice, "This is how we do it," and then he hugged me to the left and hugged me to the right. At this point the only thing I could think of was "Please don't kiss me!"

To my relief Mohammed didn't kiss me or perform a devastating finishing move, but he did thank me and my friend for stopping by and praying with him and for his family. I still marvel at encounters like these when, in an instant, God removes all our differences and restores a glimpse of what He can do through prayer. Prayer connects us to God's love, and God's love overcomes our differences. As we pray with those on our Reach List, we connect with God's love for them, and we help them connect with God's love. These prayer experiences often take only a moment but can linger for a lifetime.

When I was in college, I attended a student missions conference in Dallas, Texas. At the end of one of the sessions, we grouped together in huddles of three to four and were given the name of a university campus minister for whom to pray. Our group received the name "Mrs. Farmer" from Langston University in Langston, Oklahoma. I was excited because I was acquainted with Mrs. Farmer and was happy to pray for her and her work with college students.

After the conclusion of that session, in a very crowded hallway, I happened to spot Mrs. Farmer. Dressed in vibrant colors, she was a petite woman with a delightful, open demeanor. I went up to her to let her know our group had just prayed for her. Upon briefly sharing this with her, she gently pulled me close and said, "Let me pray for you right now!"

I nervously began thinking, *Right here? Right now? Everyone will see. This is a really crowded place. My friends might wonder what's wrong with me.* But all of these concerns and insecurities were quickly washed away as she called out to God to empower me, fill me, provide for me, protect me, and help me be the man

God wanted me to be. It was as if Mrs. Farmer pried open the lid to my soul with that prayer and poured the Spirit of God in until I was full and overflowing. That is one of the first times I remember someone praying for me like that. Immediately, spontaneously, personally praying that God would work in my life. Mrs. Farmer showed me the power of praying for and with someone in this fashion, and it was beautiful. Since that experience I have prayed with many people in many different settings and have continued to experience God's pleasure. And so can you. One thing I have learned by praying for and with people is that prayer immediately brings God into the picture, and God changes everything.

How It Works and Why It Matters

When we pray for someone by name, we don't forget their name. Something else also happens when we pray for someone by name: God begins to increase our love for them. We start thinking about their spiritual well-being. As their names are written on the palms of God's hands when we pray for them, God begins to write their names on our hearts.

As our genuine compassion for them grows, we become more aware of God's activity in their lives and how God wants to use our relationship with them. Through prayer God opens new ways for us to get to know them and new ways for them to experience His presence through how we interact with them.

Through prayer God removes barriers and opens opportunities that were not there or *were* there, but we couldn't see them. As you pray for the people on your Reach List, God begins to manifest Himself in those relationships. In that moment of intercession, the Holy Spirit reaches through our prayers to touch their spirit and begin to awaken them to the presence of God. When you share prayer with another person, God is present. As you pray with people, you will discover that many times people will have an emotional response to the experience. I used to think that they were responding to me and the words I was saying. Now I understand they were not responding to me; they were responding to the presence of God. People are often caught off guard when they encounter His presence.

If we applied naval radar to our relationships with others, at first there is only one blip on their radar. When we get to know them by name and they get to know us by name, another blip appears. When we pray with another person, a third blip appears on the radar, and that blip is God. A really cool thing about praying with another person is that after our blip has disappeared and we have departed, God's blip remains and goes with them. That encounter becomes evidence of God's presence and work in their lives.

So let's pray!

The Practical: How to Pray for Others

TIP #1 Get to know people by name and add them to your Reach List. Praying for someone by name makes it personal—and spiritually powerful—because you immediately bring God into the relationship. You can do this!

TIP #2 Pull out your Reach List and look at the first name on it. Think about how you know them. Think about some of the challenges they face. Think about them walking with Jesus and experiencing His joy, His love, and His presence.

TIP #3 Begin by praying privately for that person on your list. Here is how I begin to pray for them:

Based on Jesus' prayer in John 17, I pray the three Ps for each person by name for at least three days.

1. Pray God's **Protection**: *God, I pray that you would protect* _____ *(name).*

2. Pray God's **Provision:** *God, I pray that you would provide for* _____ *(name) and give them wisdom in all the decisions they have to make every day.*

3. Pray for **Personal Relationship:** *God, I pray that* _____ *(name) would personally come to know Jesus, love Jesus, and follow Jesus.*

TIP #4 Pray the three Ps for each person on your Reach List privately, in a place you can voice your prayer out loud. This will prepare you to pray with them.

TIP #5 Preplan your conversation in three parts. *First*, plan your approach. *Second*, plan your prayer. *Third*, plan your departure. Read the sample script below, personalize it in your own words, and practice until it sounds natural.

Hello (John/Jane), how are things going? **Listen and respond in small talk.** *(John/Jane), thank you for sharing. It was good to connect with you today. I know you have things to do today and so do I, but before we go let's pray. . . .* **Pray the three Ps personally for them as you have been praying privately for them. Your prayer should be short and personal. After the amen:** *Thanks for letting me pray with you, (John/Jane), and I hope you have a wonderful day.*

TIP #6 I used to ask permission to pray for people and how I could best pray for them. Then I realized I was creating unnecessary barriers. They would have to run the gauntlet of giving permission and coming up with something on the spot. I realized I already knew how to pray for them (the three Ps) and the easiest way to get to the moment of prayer was to simply say "LET'S PRAY." Practice praying with those closest to you to gain confidence, then branch out to pray with others with whom you are less familiar. Your confidence will grow as you pray with more and more people.

TIP #7 If praying with another person seems way out there for you, then write a card and deliver it to them. I have found this works great with busy people. I get a card and write something along these lines,

> Hello John, I wanted to encourage you today. I wanted you to know that I have personally been praying for you. I have been praying that God would protect you, that God would provide for you, and that God would give you wisdom for the decisions you make every day. I have been praying that you would come to know Jesus personally. I hope this is an encouragement to you. Your Friend, _____.

Whether you are an extrovert or introvert, there is a way to make disciples. It's your job to find the way that works best for you and do it.

TIP #8 As you pray with people, some will share specific or personal needs. When this happens, pray for them at that moment! Make a note and keep a brief list of your specific prayer requests or answers by their names. This will help you connect them to God as your relationship develops.

TIP #9 Share with other people how to pray for and with others. Making disciples requires sharing what we learn with others. If we are not sharing with others, we are not making disciples. Jesus said part of disciple making is "teaching them to obey everything I have commanded you" (Matthew 28:20).

Challenge

Add one name to your Reach List. Select a person on your Reach List and go pray with them, or write them a prayer card and give it to them. Teach one other person how to pray the three Ps.

Principle 4

This Is for You

Create Relational Breakthroughs

Getting to know someone by name makes disciple making personal. Praying for and with people makes disciple making spiritually powerful. Showing people we care makes God's love tangible! David the giant slayer declared, "Taste and see that the LORD is good" (Psalm 34:8). The good you do because you love Jesus and love people becomes the salt and light that enables people to taste and see that Jesus is good, that He is worth following with wholehearted devotion.

The greatest message ever preached, known as the Sermon on the Mount, is found in the gospel of Matthew (chapters 5-7). In it, Jesus makes an astounding declaration to his followers: "You are the salt of the earth. . . . You are the light of the world" (Matthew 5:13-14). This is a magnificent declaration of truth that describes God's intended purpose for His followers. *We were made to do good*, for we are God's works of art, original creations, commissioned and created by Jesus Christ to express His good through doing good. This is our part to play in God's eternal masterwork (Ephesians 2:10). Through doing good we become brilliant brush strokes in God's Sistine Chapel.

Jesus unveils these two powerful word pictures to help us understand how important it is to do good. Then He uncovers the ultimate purpose for the good we do. First, He says, "You are the salt of the earth." Allow His declaration to soak past surface-level knowledge and let it seep deep into your soul. Swallow it, breath it deep into your lungs, and allow it to fill you with life and purpose. Take it all the way in by personalizing His declaration over you. Write your first name in the blank below and say it aloud.

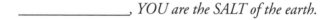

_____, *YOU are the SALT of the earth.*

Imagine Jesus looking into your eyes and personally declaring these words over you: "You are the salt of the earth."

Salt makes good food better, it makes bland food tastier, and it also makes us thirsty. Clearly capture the importance of salt. **SALT = Doing Good,** because we love God and love people. Doing good makes good relationships better, doing good makes bland relationships tastier, and doing good makes people thirsty for Jesus. Stay salty, my friends.

The second word picture Jesus proclaims over us is: "You are the light of the world." When Jesus makes a declaration, He brings immediate clarity to our purpose on this planet. He is not saying this is what you can do or should do; He is declaring the soul-fused essence of who you are as His redeemed creation. Personalize His declaration. Write your first name in the blank below and say it aloud. Jesus is declaring this over you and me every day we live.

_____, *YOU are the LIGHT of the world.*

Doing good can light up a city, doing good can light up a family, and doing good can shine light on a greater good. **LIGHT = Doing Good,** because we love God and love people. Doing good can allow a city to experience God's love. Doing good can allow a family to experience God's love. Doing good can enable others to praise God for His love.

In the same way, shine your light in clear view of people so they can see the good you do and praise your Father in heaven. (author's paraphrase of Matthew 5:16)

One of the greatest challenges about the declaration Jesus made is simply believing it. How many people do you know who get up in the morning and look in the mirror and declare with truth and vigor, "I am the salt of the earth, I am the light of the world"? Somehow that just sounds egotistical, arrogant, prideful, grandiose, and a bit unbelievable. Yet, that is who Jesus says you are! It's hard to live what you don't believe. It's not until we truly believe who Jesus says we are that we can live like it. Jesus didn't make a mistake with He pronounced that declaration over us. He was letting us know this is who we really are—who God crafted us to be. Take Jesus at His word and believe you are the salt of the earth and the light of the world so you can live like it. Being salt and light display a great purpose in God's plan.

So what does it mean to be salt and light? It means God has many good things for you to do. Don't let personal insecurity about how you think about yourself rob you of the purpose God has for you. The purpose of doing good and showing people we care is so people will look to God, thank Him, praise Him, and love Him. Stay shiny, my friends. "You are the light of the world."

In this session we are going to work on sharpening the disciple-making skill of "Showing People We Care" so they can personally taste and see that the Lord is good.

Sometimes we approach disciple making like speed dating. I have a well-meaning friend who wants to be a full-time minister. We sat down for coffee and conversation and had a spirited discussion about the life and responsibilities that full-time ministry brings. It was a good, honest, uplifting, and challenging conversation. The heart of ministry beats with love for God and love for people. If the attributes of loving God and loving people are not flowing through your veins, then full-time ministry is not something you need to pursue.

During our conversation my friend revealed that new neighbors had just moved in a couple of doors down from him. Thinking aloud about what he should do, he said, "Maybe I should just go over to their apartment and share the gospel with them." This is the Christian equivalent of speed dating. Let's forgo exchanging names, small talk, getting to know them, praying for them; let's just start kissing. More times than not, this kind of approach is not going to end well. To top it off, because our approach is so poor, we are very likely to falsely accuse them of being closed to the gospel, not loving Jesus, or even persecuting us for our faith. How we approach people has a lot to do with how we are received and how our message is received.

I suggested that my friend bring a small wrapped gift, introduce himself, and welcome his new neighbors. We need to let people know that we care personally about them. This may seem like a small, insignificant act, but it leaves lasting results and opens the door for many future conversations. It's much easier to have meaningful conversations when people know you care about them.

When we moved into our neighborhood a couple of years ago, my wife and kids delivered homemade cupcakes and brief handwritten notes to our new neighbors. This opened the way for many meaningful conversations about God, praying for their families, and comforting them during difficult times. **Are you ready for a breakthrough?** Show people you personally care for them.

Sure, there are times when we have the opportunity to share the love of Jesus with people as Phillip shared the gospel with the man from Ethiopia (Acts 8), and we need to make the most of those opportunities. However, if they move in next door to you and their first impression of you is you are *that person* who tried to cram a fistful of spiritual platitudes down their throat, chances are from that moment on they are going to avoid you like the plague of doom. Take a little time, be considerate, and show people you care. It makes the gospel sweeter and it is actually quite fun. And 1 Peter 2:15 says, it is God's will that we quiet the critics by the good we do.

Showing people you care happens in the stride of life. One day my wife and I went in a local grocery store to pick up a few items. This was intended as a quick in-and-out mission. As we were walking down one of the aisles, however, we couldn't help but notice a frazzled young mother of twins pushing one cart and pulling another. Janice said, "I remember those days." Being the parents of twins, we both could relate to the enormous struggle of trying to manage twin babies and keep a family going.

Trying to accomplish the simplest of errands with twins becomes a monumental, overwhelming proposition. It feels like someone who has stage fright being asked to be the half-time entertainment for the Super Bowl, and then having to personally pay for it. The mother of multiples who dares to go out often provides the public entertainment at personal expense.

Understanding this, we pulled alongside of her two-buggy train to offer verbal support. We told her we, too, have twins and that we had made it through the hard early years and so would she. We shared a couple brief twin stories and some laughs together and then started to get back to shopping. Showing you care can be as simple as acknowledging the struggles that someone is going through.

We took a few steps and then decided that we could make time to be of real help to her. We approached her again and asked if we could assist her. A deep look of distressed hope crossed her face.

We recommended that I could push one cart and my wife could push the other; that way, she could take her time. She looked at us in disbelief, as if to say, "Are you serious?" We assured her we would be happy to do it. With thankful apprehension, she grabbed hold of our offer. We pushed the shopping buggies and entertained the babies while this relieved young mother could take her time and do the shopping she needed to do.

We followed her up and down the aisles, helped her check out, and sacked her groceries. We then took the groceries to her car, loaded them, and even put her twins in their car seats. I had become very good at strapping children into car seats. Like a world-champion calf roper securing his calf in record time, I could strap those babies in fast and secure.

After everything was done, I closed the door and this young woman looked at us and said, "You have no idea how much this means to me." Then she closed the distance and gave me a great big strong hug full of relief and gratitude. I was glad that my wife was present or this might have been a really awkward and rather hard-to-explain moment. Next she hugged my wife with equal enthusiasm, got in her car, and drove away. Showing you care is taking action that genuinely helps another person. Doing this kind of good creates relational breakthroughs and shouts God's love.

Showing you care often begins by taking a personal interest in someone. This intentional action sounds insignificant, but it is extremely powerful when applied. So many times when we go someplace, we are going there for something we need or something we want. That is why taking a personal interest in others is often overlooked and left undone. It's just not on our mind to enter public space with the intention of taking a personal interest in someone. That is why it often takes premeditated, intentional effort to show people we care.

I have a good friend who practices taking an interest in others as well as anyone I know. Once he went into a restaurant on a Wednesday evening. Upon entering the restaurant, he noticed one of the employees with whom he had become acquainted. Judging by the look on her face, she had obliviously had a burdensome shift.

My friend approached her and said, "Looks like you have had a challenging evening."

"The hardest nights to work are Sundays and Wednesdays," she responded. "There is no tougher crowd to deal with than church people."

"I'm sorry to hear that. You know, you have always done a great job when I have been here. Tell you what, I'm going to go online and write you a favorable review."

She was amazed that someone would not only try to cheer her up but also actually do something that would benefit her.

As promised, my friend wrote a glowing review. The next time he came into the restaurant, she made a point to come by his table, sit down for a moment, and personally thank him for his review and encouragement. Since that time, she has started coming to the church where he pastors. She brings her children and encourages her friends to come as well.

Another key to showing people you care is doing good things that truly benefit them. Consider the people you normally pass and get to know their names. One of the easiest ways to show people God cares is to show people *you* care. So begin to pray for them and look for tangible ways to share God's love.

How It Works and Why It Matters

Showing we care for those on our Reach List creates breakthrough moments in our relationships. The good we do in the lives of others becomes the salt and light that allows people to taste and see that Jesus is good. I looked at every encounter Jesus had with another person and found He often did good in their lives. Through His example I found two rules for doing good.

Rule #1

Do good that truly and immediately benefits people and their situation in life. When Jesus did good to others, their life was immediately better.

Rule #2

Do good that honors God. The good Jesus did honored his heavenly Father.

How many of the people for whom Jesus did good contributed back to His ministry? It's hard to think of a clear example, and that is the point. Jesus didn't do good in someone's life so they would contribute back to His ministry. Rather, He did good in their life because He wanted to give them something that could change their life. Often after Jesus did good for someone, you will read something like this: "and the people praised God." This is the essence of being who God says we are and doing what He has given us the wherewithal to do.

By its very nature, salt adds flavor; and by its very nature, light shines. Jesus declared you are the salt of the earth and the light of the world. So add flavor to your relationships and shine God's love on your relationships. God makes His love for us known this way: while we were selfish and sinful, Jesus *gave* His life for us (Romans 5:8). The gift of Jesus has created a breakthrough for us to come to God and live new lives. Likewise, the good God has for us to do can create breakthroughs for others to come to know and praise God for the gift of His Son. The goal is that they experience God through the good we do.

The Practical: How to Show People You Care

TIP #1 Look over your Reach List and think about the people you know and the needs they have. Reflect on some of the things they have shared with you. What needs do they have and how could you meet those needs?

TIP #2 Jesus never dropped a million drachma (dollars) on anyone. Most of His encounters were simple exchanges. He spoke into their lives or He touched them, and through those simple words and actions, God's power was released.

TIP #3 Choose one of these ideas to get you started:

1. Write a personal note or handwritten card.
2. Make a phone call, send an email, or send a text.
3. Do a service project (rake leaves, wash cars, or load the dishwasher).
4. Give a simple gift (I find gift cards are great). All you need to say is "This is for you," then offer them what you have to give them.
5. Invite them to coffee, lunch, or dinner.
6. Let them know you appreciate their friendship, work, or effort.
7. Find a felt need and meet it.

TIP #4 Do good for a place of business or group by supplying them with refreshments. For example, I know about a place of business that loves a certain type of doughnuts, so once every few months, I'll bring them some.

TIP #5 Practice showing you care where you live. Put in a load of laundry, help with homework, or spend some individual time investing in your closest relationships. Sometimes we overlook those we are closest to.

TIP #6 Practice doing good for the people you work with. What are some things they enjoy? Invest in your work relationships. Be salt and light where you work.

TIP #7 Listen to what people are sharing with you. They are giving you snapshots of their lives, which offers obvious opportunities to do good.

TIP #8 When someone shares a problem with you, often there is an opportunity for good to be done. Pray about how you can bring good into their life.

Getting to know someone by name makes disciple making personal. Praying for and with people makes disciple making spiritually powerful. Showing people we care makes God's love tangible! Jesus asked people, "What would you like me to do for you?" We can ask people, "What can I do for you?"

Don't get tired of doing good, because at just the right time you will receive bountiful blessings, so don't give up. (author's paraphrase of Galatians 6:9)

Challenge

Add one name to your Reach List. Select a person on your Reach List and do good in their life. Teach another person about doing good and encourage them to do good for someone.

Principle 5

Let Me Share a Story; Tell Me Your Story

Share Stories to Build Connections

"Let me share a story." This is a powerful disciple-making phrase that can be used to inspire people to see, hear, think about, and walk with God. Sharing your story is a skill you can develop that gives flight to the disciple-making process.

In disciple making there are basically four types of stories we can share to inspire people to think about Jesus. First, there is God's Story from Genesis' "In the beginning" to Revelation's "Amen." Second, there is your salvation story: how you personally came to believe and follow Jesus Christ. Third, there are your everyday stories of how God has interacted with you throughout your life. Fourth, we can share God's stories from the Bible.

God's Story

Let's talk about how to share God's story with people on your Reach List. On a scale from zero to ten, how would you rate the complexity of the Bible (zero meaning super simple and ten meaning impossible to comprehend)?

Has anyone ever shared with you what the Bible is all about? Let me share with you three words that capture the main message of the Bible: God's REDEEMING LOVE! Let me show you how all the books in the Bible break down into bite-size portions and reveal that the Bible is about God's redeeming love.

In Genesis

God created people so we could love Him, love each other, and take care of this earth. Instead of loving God, people fell into sin, self-centeredness, and unbelief. This sin separated all people from God and has brought pain, evil, and death into the world. To set things right, God promised to send a Savior to redeem us and make things right.

In Genesis through Malachi

God used prophets, kings, and the Law as well as ongoing oppression, captivity, and deliverance as signposts pointing us to the Savior He promised to send.

In the Gospels

God sent Jesus, the long-awaited Savior who came into the world to save us from our sin and redeem us back to loving God and loving each other. Jesus is the Savior who fulfills all the prophecies and requirements in the Old Testament. He was born of a virgin, He lived a sinless life, He healed the sick, raised the dead, worked all kinds of miracles, and taught us how to love God and love people. Jesus was crucified, died, and was buried. But He rose from death on the third day. God loved us so much that He gave us His Son. Jesus loved us so much that He willingly gave His life to pay our debt of sin and redeem us back to loving God and loving each other.

In Acts through Jude

God empowered Jesus' disciples. They dedicated their lives to announce to the world that Jesus is God's promised Savior and that He alone can save us from our sins and redeem us back to loving God and loving each other.

In the Book of Revelation

God completes the process of redemption. Jesus comes back, conquers evil forever, and calls any and every person who believes and loves Him to share in the eternal love that God had intended from the very beginning. God loved the world in such an incredible way that He gave His one and only Son Jesus Christ, so that anyone who believes in Him will not perish, but rather through Him they have eternal life (John 3:16). The Bible is the story of God's redeeming love and you and I are a part of it.

Now let's talk about how to share our salvation story with those on our Reach List. In Acts 26, Paul, a follower of Jesus, shared his salvation story with a king named Agrippa. He was considerate and respectful, and he began by sharing the way he used to live (Acts 26:1-8). Next, Paul shared his life-changing encounter with Jesus (vv. 9-18). Then, he shared with King Agrippa how that encounter with Jesus changed his life forever. (vv. 19-26). Paul concludes with this statement: "King Agrippa, do you believe the prophets?

I know you do" (v. 27). Life before Jesus, life-changing encounter with Jesus, life since Jesus, and a call for others to consider following Jesus. This is a great pattern for us to use when we share our salvation story with others. The gospel flows freely when you tell your story to others, and it is super easy to share. All you have to say is "Let me share a story" and off you go. Here is my story.

My Story

Life before Jesus

I grew up in a small town in Oklahoma as the youngest of five children. My parents were divorced early on, so I have no memory of their interacting in the home as husband and wife.

After the divorce my dad gained custody of five children. He worked hard and did the best he could to raise us with the help of his mother. My grandmother, Hanna May Haynes, was a kind, hardworking, and generous woman. At one point, however, she developed Alzheimer's and could no longer help care for us. Again my dad was left to try and raise five children by himself.

I grew up like a lot of boys—running around a small rural town. I enjoyed hunting, fishing, playing sports, riding motorcycles, swimming, chasing girls, and looking for interesting things to do. Overall I had very little supervision and often found myself in trouble.

Life-Changing Encounter with Jesus

Early one Sunday morning when I was twelve years old, the telephone rang. It was an old black rotary-dial phone that the phone company rented to customers.

"Is this little Warren?" the voice asked.

"Yes."

It was a neighbor named Connie Roberts. Connie was in her seventies and she owned and operated a local restaurant. She invited me to come to Sunday school with her. She told me that if I would go to Sunday school with her, she would fix me breakfast. My eyes quickly darted around the house. Everyone was still asleep and I knew no one was going to get up and fix me anything. I wasn't sure what we had food to eat anyway. So I gladly accepted her offer, threw on the same clothes I had been wearing for the last few days, and ran to her house.

When I knocked on her door, she invited me into her warm house with wonderful smells coming from the kitchen. She told me she was glad I had come over and she began to put the food in front of me. I believe that morning we had eggs, bacon, and Post Toasties cereal. We sat around a table that had chrome legs and skirting and a floral Formica top with matching chairs. As we sat and ate, she began to share with me stories and phrases from the Bible.

From that day on, Connie Roberts was my friend. We shared many meals and many Bible lessons together. I started looking for ways to help her. I started mowing her lawn, washing dishes at her restaurant, and picking up around her yard.

It was at her table over a bowl of cereal that Connie helped me understand why Jesus came to earth and what He did for me. She taught me these words of our Savior from the Bible: For God so loved the world, that he gave his only begotten Son, that whoever believeth in him should not perish, but have everlasting life (John 3:16 KJV).

Through this Bible verse Connie helped me personalize the love God has for me. She told me that God loves me and that Jesus died for me! As a twelve-year-old boy, with the help of Connie and a pastor, I asked Jesus to forgive my sins and committed to follow Him for the rest of my life.

Life since Jesus

There was an immediate change. The next day I started talking about Jesus to my friends at school. I began to try to live to please Him. I noticed He was always with me in my mind. He even spoke to me in my thoughts. My outlook and desires began to change. I wanted to clean up my language, stop lying, and quit stealing.

There was a new joy, excitement, and hope inside of me. I wanted to try to help other people. Little did I know that a phone call early on a Sunday morning, along with the prospect of an easy breakfast, would impact my entire life and future. I have spent my life trying to help people know the forgiveness, hope, and joy that I received from Jesus.

Call for Others to Consider Jesus

Have you ever personalized the forgiveness and love Jesus has for you? We can use everyday life stories where God has saved and rescued us to help and encourage others.

While I was working on this book in a local coffee shop, I was talking with a new friend of mine who has worked as an attorney for years. He learned I was in the ministry and began to talk with me about an inspirational attraction located just a few miles from where we lived. The Shrine of Christ's Passion is located in St. John, Indiana, and is a beautiful portrayal of all Jesus has done for us.

The Shrine of Christ's Passion is filled with stunning craftsmanship and powerful displays of life-size bronze recreations of the trial, crucifixion, death, burial, and resurrection of Jesus Christ. My friend was trying to encourage me to take some time and visit the Shrine with my family. Then he shared with me a God story.

He said that once while he was walking through the different scenes, there was a Hispanic family a little farther in front of him. There was a mother, a father, and two bouncy little raven-haired girls. They had moved ahead to the next scene. When his family rounded the corner, there was Jesus staggering under the burden of the cross. He watched as those two little girls ran to Jesus and hugged Him as He struggled under the weight.

As you can imagine, he choked up as he relived that beautiful moment. Then he said, "You really do need to go and see it." Believe me, after his story, I wanted to immediately take my family to go see it. A well-told God story can move people to personally hear, see, think about, and experience Jesus.

The next day I met with a longtime friend. I told him about this story. He asked me if I knew why the financier had poured millions of dollars into building the Shrine of Christ's Passion. When I answered no, he said it was because this man had lost his daughter in a car accident. This man was so inspired by God's giving His Son to redeem a lost and dying world that he in turn redeemed the loss of his beloved daughter. He transformed a devastating personal tragedy into an opportunity to triumph and inspire countless people to personally experience the Passion of Jesus Christ.

We can also tell stories from the Bible. There are countless intriguing stories that we can share with others. Missionaries all over the world use Bible stories to communicate to new cultures. The great thing about these stories is once you learn them you can take them with you everywhere you go. I have shared Bible stories over the counter, sitting next to someone in a coffee shop, and in conversations with neighbors. I was introduced to a wonderful resource that I will pass on to you. All you have to do is go to https://bible.org/series/all-stories-bible. There you will have immediate access to 255 Bible stories written by John Walsh, a masterful storyteller.

One suggestion you might consider is to select three to four stories from the Bible and work on sharing those with your family and friends. I tend to share stories about Jesus. The account of Jesus being trusting God through times of temptation (Matthew 4:1-11), Jesus forgives sin (Mark 2:1-12), Jesus walking on water (Matthew 14:22-32), and Jesus inviting Himself over for dinner with Zacchaeus (Luke 19:1-9) are all good ones to start with.

Storytelling is a skill we can develop and use to help people see, hear, think about, and experience Jesus. All Scripture is inspired by God and is useful for teaching, putting a stop to bad behavior, straightening us out, and preparing us to live right with God and people so that we will be whole and ready to do the good work God has for us to do (2 Timothy 3:16-17).

How It Works and Why It Matters

Sharing stories does three amazing things in our relationships with others. First, stories create room in the lives of others for us and our message and create room in our lives for them. Every time we share stories, we carry a little of each other with us. Second, stories inspire action. Personal experience is the most powerful agent for affecting change. A well-told story is the second most powerful motivator we can use. A well-told story allows a person to vicariously experience an event with their mind and emotions without having personally been there. Third, sharing stories builds relational connections, like synapses firing to create clear passages in our brains or Mr. Miyagi from *The Karate Kid* building muscle memory. Sharing stories builds connections with those we share them with.

The key phrase for sharing your stories is "Let me share a story." The key phrase to get them to tell their story is "Tell me your story."

The Practical: How to Share Your Stories

TIP #1 Look over your Reach List and ask one person on the list to share their story with you.

TIP #2 By this time in the disciple-making journey, we have built a solid relational framework. We have come to know people by name, we have prayed for and with them, and we have shown them that we personally care about them. Once people know or sense we care about them, they become open to truly receiving the stories we share.

TIP #3 Think about sharing stories in four parts.

1. **Create interest.** A show of concern, a thought-provoking statement, a question, a scenario, a sense of common ground, or a shared experience can spring you into your story.

2. **Start your story.** *Let me share a story.* I have used this statement to tell many stories through the years. This statement helps you transition into telling your story.
3. **Keep it brief.** Work on sharing your stories in about three minutes. All the stories I have shared with you in this book only take a few minutes to share. Keeping our stories brief allows us to share them in more settings.
4. **Inspire people.** I believe the primary reason for sharing our God stories is to inspire people to love God and love people. Think about your story and ask yourself, *If someone shared this story with me, what would it inspire me to do?*

TIP #4 Write out God's story, your salvation story, and one life story. A friend of mine once told me, "If you haven't written it out, you haven't thought it through." Use the speech to text on your cell phone or computer to write your stories.

TIP #5 Practice sharing God's story, your salvation story, a life story, and a biblical story with a willing family member or friend. Time yourself and ask for honest feedback. Sharing your stories is a skill that takes time and practice to sharpen. You can also record yourself telling your story, listen, and make adjustments until it flows.

TIP #6 Share God's story from Genesis to Revelation, share your salvation story, share one of your life stories, and share a Bible story with people on your list. Share one of the stories per person. Call them up or meet them for coffee. Ask them how everything is going. Listen, then say, "I want to encourage you today. Let me share a story with you." Then you're off and running.

TIP #7 It's important not to do all the talking. Make sure you ask them to share part of their story with you. I will often say, "Tell me a story from your life." They are an expert on their life, and many people are happy to share about themselves.

TIP #8 Keep praying, showing that you care, and sharing your stories with people on your list.

TIP #9 Share what you have learned about sharing your stories with other people. Making disciples requires sharing what we learn with others. If we are not sharing with others, we are not making disciples.

TIP #10 Sharing your God stories can inspire people to hear, see, feel, think about, and experience God's forgiveness, peace, strength, and love. Your stories can help their faith grow and help people believe God for greater things. God can use every story we share to inspire someone He loves. God can use your stories to change someone's life. Share your stories.

Challenge

Ask one person, "What's your name?" and write on your Reach List where you met them. Ask one person to share their story with you: "Share that story with me." Share one of the four stories with someone on your list by saying, "Let me share a story with you." By sharing your story, you are teaching and inspiring others to think about Jesus.

Principle 6

With Me

How to Move People Spiritually

W*ith me.* This may be one of the most profound and powerful disciple-making practices I have discovered. I am going to share with you how you can move people spiritually. First of all, I didn't even know that was possible or legal. You are going to learn how you can move people to take spiritual steps and how incredibly simple that process is.

A personal invitation is a powerful invitation. Notice how personal the invitation was that Jesus gave to the men He was recruiting to be His disciples.

As Jesus was walking beside the Sea of Galilee, he spotted two brothers, Simon who was also called Peter and his brother Andrew. They were casting a net into the lake, for they were fishermen. "Come, follow me," Jesus said, "and I will send you out to fish for people." At once they left their nets and followed him. (Matthew 4:18-20)

Let's look at how developing the skill of giving personal invitations can enhance our disciple-making effectiveness. We will use Jesus as our model for learning how to give personal invitations. According to His example, disciple making happens in the stride of everyday life. It happened "as Jesus was walking beside the Sea" (v. 18).

Think about the people God has brought into your everyday life. List the names and contact information for people you see on a regular basis. This list of names forms your Reach List and clarifies the people whom you are most likely to influence for Jesus. Don't forget to set a personal goal to add at least one new person to your list every week.

You will find it doesn't take long before you are personally living these words: "As I was walking along, I met . . ." As you go about your day, you will discover ample opportunities to get to know people you can begin a disciple-making relationship with.

Another important aspect of giving personal invitations is knowing people by name. Jesus "spotted two brothers, Simon called Peter and his brother Andrew" (v. 18). Jesus not only knew both their names, but He also knew that they were brothers. Knowing people by name makes your invitations personal. When I meet someone new I add their names and where I met them to my list. This helps me remember them and it also makes it possible for me to pray for them and personally interact with them in a much more personal way.

Have you ever noticed how easy it is to walk by someone you don't know and how difficult it is to walk by someone that you do know by name without interacting with them in some way? Get in the habit of calling people by name; this helps us live out what we see modeled in this passage by Jesus.

Notice that Jesus also knew what they did: "They were fishermen" (v. 18). This was easy to discern, because at that moment they were actually fishing. These are what I call "snapshots" (pieces of personal information that can build relational integrity). There is nothing more important in life than relationships. When people share information about themselves, it is an act of trust. God is trusting us and they are trusting us. "Snapshots" build and strengthen our social relationships. When we are able to call someone by name and draw attention to something he is interested in, we are in a fabulous position to begin to influence them toward Jesus.

Think about the people on your Reach List. What are a few "snapshots" you know about them? Write them by their names and remember—this is a trust. If we use any information to gossip or cause hurt, we have broken trust. Do not under any circumstances let any unwholesome words and conversations come out of your mouths, but speak only what is helpful for building others up according to their needs. Let your conversations truly benefit those who listen (author's paraphrase of Ephesians 4:29).

When Jesus gave His invitation to Peter and Andrew, He didn't invite them to an event or place. He invited them to Himself: "Come, follow me" (Matthew 4:19). We can learn much from this example. The point of a personal invitation is for us to draw people to ourselves, not to a place or event. Jesus' invitation to these two brothers was for them to come into relationship with Him and be a part of His life. Personal relationships are the plutonium that is needed for explosive disciple making.

For years I focused on the secondary invitation. Growing up in church I have heard for years you need to be "fishers of men," so I told people that they should be "fishers of men" (Matthew 4:19 KJV). It wasn't until I realized that fishing for people was the secondary invitation and was completely dependent on the primary invitation, which is to follow Jesus. The motion of the text in what Jesus literally said in Matthew was: "Follow me and **through relationship with me** I will make you fishers of men" (author's paraphrase and emphasis). Discipleship is relationally driven.

Let's look at a common approach to giving a general or generic invitation, and then we will contrast that with a personal invitation. One common invitation is "Come to church" or "I want to invite you to church." These two invitations are processed the same, as a general invitation to a place. The thing we need to understand about general invitations is that people generally do not respond to them.

In disciple making we need to re-personalize our invitations the way Jesus did. Instead of saying, "I want you to come to church," look them in the eye and say, "I want you to come to church with me. What do you say?" The words *with me* are the key; they are what make the invitation personal. A personal invitation is not personal because you say it. It is only a personal invitation when it results in a personal relationship with you.

Our job in disciple making is to give personal invitations that will help people move closer to Jesus. **Disciple making is not all up to us!** The people we personally invite must respond in order for relationships to develop. Notice how Peter and Andrew responded: At once they left their nets to follow Him (Matthew 4:20). Because disciple making is relational in nature, we need to remember this law for building relationships. I call this law "The Law of Invitation and Response." The reason that Peter and Andrew became disciples of Jesus is because they responded to His invitation and followed Him.

Let's compare and contrast the response of Peter and Andrew with that of the rich young ruler. Jesus gave this young man, who was full of potential, this invitation: "If you want to be perfect, go, sell your possessions and give to the poor, and you will have treasure in heaven. Then come, follow me" (Matthew 19:21).

Peter and Andrew left their fishing business behind to follow Jesus and became His disciples. How would this man respond to the same offer? "When the young man heard this, he went away sad, because he had great wealth" (v. 22). Jesus loved this young man, but He couldn't take him any further because this young man wouldn't follow Him. We can't disciple someone who will not follow us, and neither could Jesus.

Jesus' invitation is still "Come follow me," and the only acceptable response is to follow. We are working on our disciple-making skills to share the invitation of Jesus and encourage people follow Him. A disciple of Jesus is someone who believes, loves, and follows Him. By honing the art of giving personal invitations, we can inspire people to follow us as we follow Jesus.

This is what Jesus means in the Great Commission when He says, "Go and make disciples of all nations, baptizing . . . and teaching them to obey everything I have commanded you" (28:19-20). Where does someone have to be to observe something? A person has to be present or be in position to see what's going on. If we are going to make disciples, then we need to give personal invitations to people so they can watch, hear, and personally experience what following Jesus is all about by observing us. Paul said it this way: "Follow my example, as I follow the example of Christ" (1 Corinthians 11:1).

One of the best ways we can help a person follow Jesus is by giving them personal invitations to follow us as we follow Jesus, just as Connie Roberts, my former septuagenarian neighbor, gave me a personal invitation to come eat breakfast and to go to Sunday school with her. Through that invitation I came to personalize God's love, forgiveness, and hope through the death, burial, and resurrection of Jesus Christ. It was through Connie's personal invitation and example that I came into a life-changing encounter with Jesus and committed to follow Him all the days of my life.

While I was in college, a mentor of mine personally invited me to go through a discipleship study with him. The book we used is entitled *Experiencing God: Knowing and Doing the Will of God*, by Henry Blackaby and Claude King. Through this study book and the mentorship of John Heath, I heard God calling me to preach His Word. I have had the privilege of speaking to many people through the years, and it has become my life's goal to inspire people to love God and love people.

In my junior year of college, I received a personal invitation from James Vaughn to serve as a mission pastor in Rico, Colorado. James helped disciple me by allowing me to live with his family and follow him around for two summers. James showed me what living for Jesus practically and tangibly looked like. James has been a dear friend and mentor for decades and has personally helped me think through many different blessings and challenges. When I said yes to his personal invitation, I said yes to a lifelong friendship.

On another occasion I received a personal invitation to go to Haiti to help build a house for a pastor and speak to people about God's love. I learned the Haitian phrase *Mwen kwe Jezi*, meaning "I believe Jesus." While walking one day, I met a young girl who wanted to talk to a "Blond" or a Caucasian, but she couldn't speak English and I couldn't speak Creole. So I shared with her the only phrase I knew: Mwen kwe Jezi. She smiled brightly, reached her arms to the sky, and then crossed them over her heart and said, "Mwen kwe Jezi." In that moment I deeply admired a young girl who joyfully loved Jesus just for the love of Jesus. It was beautiful!

It has taken me years to learn what I am sharing with you. Each time I accepted one of these personal invitations, I learned more about loving Jesus and loving people. I grew as a follower of Christ by saying yes to these, and many more, personal invitations. We cannot inspire people to follow Jesus without giving them personal invitations to follow us as we follow Christ. The beautiful revelation is that with every personal invitation we give, we embrace an opportunity to deepen our love for Jesus and for those He brings into our lives.

How It Works and Why It Matters

This may be one of the most powerful skills we can develop. Learning to give personal invitations is how we move people spiritually from here to there. When Jesus wanted to move fishermen, doctors, and IRS workers to become followers, He gave them a personal invitation. Think about what Jesus literally said to them:

"Come, follow me, and I will show you how to fish for people!" (Matthew 4:19 NLT). Notice that the primary invitation was to relationship, and through relationship with Himself, He would introduce them to a world they couldn't know without Him. An invitation is not personal because we say it. It is personal because it leads to a personal relationship with us, just as it leads to a personal relationship with Jesus. The key phrase to giving a personal invitation is "with me!"

Here is how it works. Say you're making a general announcement inviting people to come to a workday at church. If you have given many of these, you already know the response is going to be limited. Why? Because the only thing people are considering is whether doing yard work at church is more important than everything else in their life. Now imagine you approach three people personally and say, "Would you come to the workday *with me?*" Now their primary consideration is their relationship with you, and their secondary consideration is the workday.

A well-delivered personal invitation causes people to weigh relationship with you first, not a certain activity. Relationship is what empowers the personal invitations we give. These personal invitations we extend to others form a well-lit path to help them discover Jesus.

You move people at the rate you give personal invitations. If you want to see God working once a month, then give a personal invitation once a month. If you want to see God at work throughout your day, then give personal invitations throughout your day and you will find that God is not afraid to work you. He will give you all you want.

The Practical: How to Give Personal Invitations

TIP #1 Select a person on your Reach Llist and give them a personal invitation using the words *with me*!

TIP #2 Personalize your invitations by using a phrase like "I would like you to have (coffee, lunch, a get-together, etc.) with me."

TIP #3 Keep a list of "snapshots" for the people on your Reach List. These "snapshots" will enhance your ability to offer personal invitations. Example: I discovered the favorite restaurant of a young woman God had brought into our lives and I invited her to have lunch with my wife and me. It's easier to give personal invitations and make connections when we know the things they are interested in.

TIP #4 Personalize your invitations by using people's names, connecting to their interests, and inviting them to share experiences with you and/or your family.

TIP #5 Knowing a person by name, praying with them, showing you care, sharing your stories, and listening to theirs will empower your personal invitations.

TIP #6 Think about what you will talk about when you get together. Think of a few questions that focus on their lives.

TIP #7 Always focus on the other person before sharing. Then say something like this: *I have been looking forward to getting to know you better. Tell me about **your** _____ (-self, work, family, story, interests, spiritual journey). Our love for others grows as we get to know them better.

TIP #8 Be aware of your surroundings. Be aware of the people that frequent the same places you do. The places you share are common ground that you can use to invest in these relationships. Give personal invitations that allow you to share personal space.

TIP #9 Avoid what I call the "one and done" mentality. Strive for multiple ongoing spiritual and relational investments. Keep giving invitations for them to share life with you.

TIP #10 Jesus is our model for life. He gave personal invitations to his disciples. Those who said yes to His invitations grew in their love for God and their love for people. We are responsible for skillfully extending personal invitations that inspire people to follow Jesus. Every personal invitation we give, we embrace an opportunity to deepen our love for Jesus and our love for others. It will require a string of personal invitations to move people toward Jesus. However, it only takes one personal invitation to connect a person to Jesus and change his life.

Challenge

Ask one person, "What's your name?" and write on your Reach List where you met them. Give a person on your list a personal invitation by saying, "(Their name) _____, I want you to come **with me** to _____. What do you say?" Teach one person how to give a personal invitation.

Principle 7

Gather People

Gather People to Influence People .

Gathering people in groups is a tremendous skill you can use to amplify your disciple-making effectiveness. There are many examples of gathering people in the Bible. For the purpose of this session I will share four specific examples of gathering people and how to use them in disciple making. Let's look to the life and practice of Jesus as our example.

First, Jesus personally gathered people one by one. While Jesus was walking along the Sea of Galilee, He saw Peter and his brother Andrew and he gave them a personal invitation. His invitation in Matthew 4:19 was simple: "Come, follow me." And they did. This put Jesus in a mentoring relationship with Peter and Andrew. On another occasion, when Jesus came across a tax collector named Matthew, again He extended a personal invitation: "Follow me and be my disciple" (9:9). And Matthew did. This put Matthew in a mentoring relationship with Jesus.

Jesus was getting ready to go to another town, and He made a decision to extend a personal invitation to Philip. This put Philip in position to be coached by Jesus. The first way to gather people is one by one, which puts us in position to mentor them in their relationship with Jesus. This doesn't mean you are stuck mentoring a person for the rest of your life. It might turn out to be a mentoring moment you can use to point someone toward Jesus. Like Jesus, create these coachable moments by inviting people into a one-on-one encounter.

Second, Jesus gathered a few friends to share a personal disciple-making experience with them. I want to draw your attention to the gathering of close personal friends. Jesus took Peter, John, and James with him to share a powerful time of prayer together (Luke 9:28-36). These three were brought into a powerful life-altering personal and spiritual encounter with Jesus and each other when He invited them to what we now call the Mount of Transfiguration.

These three formed a powerful bond with Jesus and each other. Peter never forgot this encounter and wrote about it in 2 Peter 1:18: "We ourselves heard this voice that came from heaven when we were with him on the sacred mountain." There is evidence of the strength of this bond with each other even during times of personal and spiritual failure. Consider what transpired after the crucifixion of Jesus. Peter's faith was floundering and he went back to his old life of fishing. After the resurrection Jesus personally went to Peter to coach him up and restore him from his backslidden state. Where were Peter's friends from the mountain top experience? Where were his friends when Peter was in this personal pit?

John 21 reveals that one of those friends from the mountain-top experience was were right there with him. Peter turned and looked at John, who is referred to in the passage as the disciple Jesus *loved*. There just might be a reason why he was given that designation. John was right there in eyeshot of Peter. A friend on the mountaintop with Jesus and a friend in the valley of personal despair. These types of friendships carry staying power. Like Jesus, a disciple maker can forge these kind of friendships that see us through the ups and downs of life.

I believe this type of personal gathering was championed by Jesus when He said, "Where two or three gather in my name, there I am with them" (Matthew 18:20). Like Jesus, a disciple maker can create these kind of opportunities that lead to profound friendships and spiritual transformation.

Third, Jesus gathered a little larger group of twelve. This group lived life with Jesus and one another. These men became the twelve apostles (Mark 3:13-19). They shared in Jesus' work and ministry. They listened to His sermons, experienced His miracles, persisted through persecution, shared in His sorrow, went on mission trips, and worked together to do whatever Jesus asked them to do. Like Jesus, a disciple maker can gather this kind of group.

Fourth, Jesus gathered large crowds of people. On occasion many people would gather from all over the region to experience Jesus. They wanted to share the experience of His miracles and listen to His teachings. There are many examples of large crowds coming to see Jesus.

As Jesus and His disciples were leaving Jericho, a large crowd followed Him. On this occasion they watched as Jesus healed two blind men (Matthew 20:29-34). This gave people lots to talk about when they went home. They all shared a powerful experience that worked to inspire a large number of people to follow Jesus. Like

Jesus, a disciple maker can gather people into large-group experiences that form a shared experience and fuel personal inspiration. Jesus used all of these types of gatherings to help people love God and love others. Therefore, we can gather people into these groups to inspire them to follow Jesus. I believe it is important to use all of these types of gatherings for the purpose of disciple making. We open the door for people to come closer to Jesus every time we extend a personal invitation to gather. One thing I know for sure is that Jesus was intentional about gathering people, and I believe we must be intentional about giving personal invitations to gather and move people toward Jesus as well.

How It Works and Why It Matters

A great way to maximize the skill of gathering people into these different groups is to understand spatial dynamics. First, there is the two-foot space commonly referred to as "intimate space." When we want to tell someone a secret, we draw close and whisper it in his ear. We enter "intimate space" to share information that is really important or confidential. Do you really want someone yelling across a crowded room to let you know that your fly is down?

We will only bring one person at a time into this "intimate space." This is where you fall in love with your spouse. This is where best friends hang out. This is where you make meaningful connections with people you meet. This is where you spend time with Jesus in quiet time. As a disciple maker you need to know that this is where coaching and mentoring moments are created.

Second, there is the four-foot circle known as "personal space." This is the space in which people are most likely to interact on a personal level. This is the space where we build personal friendships.

We will allow approximately three individuals into our personal space at any given time. As a disciple maker we need to understand that this is where personal discipleship happens.

Would you like to "close the back door of the church," meaning, would you like to stop people from leaving the church today? My question is, do you know where the back door of the church is? I have asked this question to countless people and have yet to get a definitive answer. Most won't even dare to venture to guess because foundationally it feels like a question we should know the answer to. Nevertheless, I am going to tell you with precision where the back door of the church is.

The number one reason people leave the church is because they do not have meaningful, lasting friendships in church. Then the question becomes, where do meaningful and lasting friendships develop? The answer to your question precisely pinpoints the back door of the church. So here goes. The back door of the church— the place where meaningful and lasting friendships are forged—is a four-foot circle called personal space. This is where you spend quantity time talking about personal and spiritual things.

As a pastor, my wife and I would invite newcomers over to our house about every six to eight weeks, as schedules allowed. We would tell them to come over on a Friday or Saturday about 3:00 or 4:00 p.m., and to bring their family and plan on letting the kids play. We'd then have dinner together and hang out until they were ready to go. They would arrive on time, the children would entertain themselves, we would share a meal, and often we would look up at the clock and it would be 10:00 or 11:00 p.m., at which point we would kick them out so I could be half coherent to speak three times the next day.

When we saw each other the following day, something was different. We were no longer acquaintances; we were friends. These friends would often stay in church until they moved or until we moved. Observing this effect, I encouraged people from the church to invite people into their homes. Because I didn't fully understand where and how friendships form, I unintentionally mislabeled and misdirected people for years. It's not having people in your homes; it's what you do there that forms friendships. We sat around a table (four-foot circle) and spent quantity time (six to eight hours) together talking about personal things (where they grew up, their hobbies, etc.) and spiritual things (whether they grew up in church, their spiritual story, etc.).

The challenge for most churches today is there is NO place or opportunity for people to get in a four-foot circle to share quantity time together talking about personal and spiritual things. There are many congregations and businesses that are intentionally or unintentionally practicing this, and they are easy to identify because they have high retention rates and build a loyal following. These first two spaces are the most neglected in congregations today, but they carry the most relational equity.

Third, there is the twelve-foot space known as "social space." Sharing this space with others is where we get to know each other on a social level. This is where we share "snapshots" of one another's lives. We learn information about each other's families, hobbies, interests, and personalities. We will share "social space" with about five to twenty people. This is where small groups happen. This space is excellent for dynamic small group discovery, training, learning, and interacting.

Fourth, there is the space beyond twelve feet known as "public space." You can fit the whole world in this space. "Public space" is where people share large-scale experiences like concerts, conferences, sporting events, rallies, television shows, and movies. In disciple making, this is where we share inspirational experiences like congregational worship, Christian concerts, evangelistic crusades, and large-scale conferences with famous presenters. Even best-selling books can become shared experiences. The important goal of a large group meeting is to create and share an encouraging and inspiring experience together that forms spiritual markers along the path to following Jesus.

We gather people to inspire them to follow Jesus. When we gather one-on-one, we create coaching and mentoring relationships to inspire people to follow Jesus. When we gather people in groups of four, we develop strong meaningful personal friendships and fuel personal discipleship experiences. When we gather people into groups of five to twenty, we fashion great small group learning environments that lead to spiritual discovery and breakthrough learning.

When we gather people into large groups of twenty or more, we share wonderful inspirational experiences together and light our path. All of these gatherings are used in disciple making. It is a mistake to think that disciple making only happens in one of these spaces. Rather, disciple making happens through your relationship with another person, and all these spaces you share become an avenue to influence and inspire them to follow Jesus.

It is important to grasp that we can inspire people to follow Jesus in all of the spaces we share with people. It is also important to know that we can move people from one space to another and create new levels of relational depth. As a disciple maker, YOU are the common factor in all of these spaces and the key to using these spaces to inspire people to love God, love others, and follow Jesus. As a follower of Jesus, YOU are a spiritual "difference maker." You can move the spiritual needle in peoples' lives. By practicing disciple-making skills like knowing people by name, building a Reach List, praying for and with people, showing them that you care, sharing your stories, giving personal invitations, and gathering them into groups, you can have a profound spiritual influence in their lives.

You are chosen by God. You were made to carry out the priestly purposes of the King. You are a nation of believers set apart for God's purposes. You belong to God. So announce Jesus to the world. Tell people about the ONE who has called you out of darkness and who has called you into HIS light and life (1 Peter 2:9). It is vital to remember we are spiritual people and we have a spiritual purpose to fulfill.

Just like Abraham was given the blessing of being a blessing, we, too, have been given the blessing of being a spiritual blessing to others. God has chosen you to make the glorious mystery of Christ known to people. What is this mystery? Christ living in you is the hope of glory (Colossians 1:27). We gather people to move them closer to Jesus and propel them toward His love and purpose for their lives. You can help people personalize Jesus Christ by gathering them into groups and sharing your stories.

Once I was driving home after evening classes, and I sensed the Spirit of God asking me to visit a man named Kevin. He had been a neighbor of mine and had recently moved. I had also built a good relationship with Kevin and his wife. My wife and I had them over to our house and had invited them to church. Kevin and I had worked out together, and we had gone hunting together. As I was driving back from my classes, I called Kevin and asked if I could stop by his house and talk with him. He said, "Sure." I knew I needed to talk with him about Jesus.

I took a deep breath and knocked on Kevin's door. He answered and invited me in. I told him the truth about what brought me to his door.

"I was driving and praying when God brought your name to mind, and I believe He wanted me to talk with you."

Kevin sat and listened carefully. (This kind of encounter doesn't happen every day, so people will often hear what you have to say.)

I shared with Kevin God's story and my story, and then I asked if he had ever personalized God's love: "Have you personally believed and committed your life to following Jesus?"

He said he had not, so I asked him if he would like to and he indicated he would. Next, I led Kevin in a simple prayer where he asked Jesus for forgiveness, acknowledged that Jesus died on the cross and rose again, and committed his life to follow Jesus. This was a powerful, spiritually charged moment. We live empowered every time we follow Jesus into these moments.

On another occasion we invited our neighbors to our house for a Bible study get-together. We prepared a fun icebreaker to help people get to know each other. My wife and girls worked on refreshments, and I worked out the details for the Bible study and group interactions. It turned out to be a wonderful experience. Even though we were new to the neighborhood, we were able to facilitate an experience that helped people get to know each other better. This has also opened up many opportunities for us to pray and provide spiritual direction for our neighbors.

As followers of Jesus, we need to take spiritual responsibility for our neighbors and the people God brings into our lives—even if this involves stepping out of our comfort zone. To accomplish God's will, we must be aware of our feelings and thoughts, particularly the presence of love and fear. Fear will always try to talk us out of doing what God wants, while love will empower us to walk in the presence, power, and love of God. "The Spirit God gave us does not make us timid, but gives us power, love and self-discipline" (2 Timothy 1:7).

I intentionally frequent the same coffee shops, restaurants, and businesses. I avoid the drive-thru and make it a point to go inside and talk with people. Being a disciple maker means we are in the people business. I keep lists of businesses, employees, and customers. I keep lists of people, their names, where I met them, and snapshots I have learned along the way. There is a vital connection between being spiritually intentional and being spiritually influential.

Cultivating awareness of our surroundings and opportunities is important to the skill of gathering groups. It's not that there are not opportunities to gather people; it's just most of the time, I don't see them. Wherever people naturally gather in the stride of life can develop into a spiritual gathering. I have friends that have started conversation groups on their lunch breaks, after work, in restaurants, at hospitals, in school bus barns, apartment complexes, sports practices, and before school groups. Any natural gathering presents an opportunity for disciple making.

In Chattanooga, Tennessee, I experienced a man who, in the early morning hours from about 6:30 to 10:00 a.m., shared one of God's stories from the Bible with three different groups. It was amazing and opened my eyes to just how unaware I had been concerning the opportunities that exist around me.

God often works through what we call "inconveniences" to position us to accomplish HIS work. For instance, I was preparing for a speaking engagement on a Sunday afternoon when a lady just plopped down in front of me. It was surprising because I didn't know her. I said hello, and she said, "I noticed your Bible and I wanted to know if you go to church." I said I did, and I let her know I would be going to church that evening. I told her where the church was and the times of the services.

She told me she lived in a hotel down the street and asked if I would pick her up and give her a ride to church. She gave me her name, phone number, and room number.

By this time, I was way out of my comfort zone. Red caution flags were out and waving with full force. My initial thoughts about this requests were: *I am really busy. How am I going to deal with this interruption? There is no way on earth I am going to go pick this woman up at a hotel.* But I told her I would do my best to get her to church.

"I'll be waiting outside at 5:45 p.m.," she said.

After she left I called my wife and told her what had just happened. She was scheduled to be at another church with our children, but said she would go if I couldn't find anyone to help. I called a wonderful young woman from the church where I was going to speak. I told her the situation and asked if she could pick up Debbie from the hotel. She graciously agreed after a hardy chuckle.

When the church service began, I looked over the audience and, sure enough, there was Debbie in front of me. After that encounter it dawned on me that this woman lived along with a number of others. She was a person of peace who could open the door to sharing God's stories with a community of people that would very likely NEVER come to an existing church.

Every person can be a pathway to gathering a group. They know people we don't know. We need to be aware of the potential in every person we meet. Every person on your Reach List is a potential group that could be gathered for the purpose of following Jesus.

The Practical: How to Gather People

TIP #1 Look at your Reach List of names and best contact information and pray for each person to be receptive to the invitations you will give them. When you are inviting someone to a group, you can leverage their friends with others by asking if they have someone they could invite.

TIP #2 Get others involved from the beginning. If you are gathering a few friends, a small group, or a large group, get others involved from the beginning. Working together can be a lot of fun and very productive. Combine your Reach Lists to form groups fast.

TIP #3 Gathering people begins with planning. Whether you are gathering one-on-one groups, a few friends, a small group, or a large group, it is important to plan. Be able to answer the following questions: why, what, when, where, and who?

1. Why are you gathering these people? Example: I want to get my neighbors together so we can get to know each other better.

2. What kind of gathering is it? Example: a neighborhood gathering.
3. When? Example: Thursday, November 7, 2015, at 7:00 p.m.
4. Where? Example: our house, located at (address and phone number).
5. Who am I going to personally invite to this gathering? Example: my ten closest neighbors.

TIP #4 Give personal "with me" invitations. Make a simple invitation card or flyer, personally deliver it, and say you want them to come with you. Send a reminder email, text, or phone call the morning of the evening event, or the evening before a morning or midday event.

TIP #5 Design the meeting. Design an encouraging, engaging, and inspirational gathering. Visualize the gathering from beginning to end. **Basic elements of a meeting to visualize are**

- welcoming guests
- refreshments
- introductions
- icebreaker
- WOW factor
- group interaction
- transitions (how you move seamlessly from one element to the next)
- sharing your story
- a Bible lesson or spiritual direction
- call to action
- conclusion

Free resources for these basic elements and activities can be downloaded onto your PC, laptop, or smartphone. In this time of technology, resources are often a click away. The ultimate goal of gathering people for the purpose of disciple making is to inspire them to follow Jesus.

TIP #6 Evaluate the effectiveness of your gathering, make any needed adjustments, and start planning your next one. Pay close attention to the details. The discoveries are in the details.

TIP #7 Don't base your effectiveness on a few attempts. It takes time to build a skill like gathering people.

TIP #8 Be aware of impromptu coaching moments that surface during your day. There are way more opportunities to gather people than we are aware of. We are just used to walking by them instead of seizing them.

TIP #9 Gathering people in groups is a tremendous skill you can use to amplify your disciple-making effectiveness.

Challenge

Ask one person, "What's your name?" and write their name on your Reach List and where you met them. Give a person on your list a personal invitation to gather with you: "(Their name) _____, I want you to come **with me** to _____. What do you say?" Teach one person the four spaces Jesus gathered people to make disciples.

Principle 8

Multiply Leaders

Empower Rapid Advance

The foundation of any growing organization, ministry, or church is built on developing leaders and reaching new people. Jesus multiplied leaders. He began by personally recruiting twelve men who were with Him as He went through all the neighborhoods and communities. They were with Him as He taught about God's kingdom. They were with Him as He shared the good news of forgiveness and redemption. They were with Him as He ministered to the sick and hurting (Matthew 9:35-36).

The Twelve soon turned into seventy-two. Jesus appointed these seventy-two disciples and sent them two by two ahead of Him into the surrounding communities to share good news and announce His coming. They went out together, worked together, and they came back celebrating together (Luke 10:1-17). There are many examples in the Bible of leaders developing others and reaching new demographics. Developing leaders and reaching new people are foundational pillars to any effective ministry.

I have sat through numerous conferences, meetings, and focus groups on church growth, and I can tell you with confidence that these two practices are essential to growing ministries and organizations. One example is Sunday school: An effective Sunday school ministry is built on starting new units or classes. What do you need to start a new unit or Sunday school class? You need a leader and you need new members. Sunday school stagnation happens when the Sunday school stops developing new leaders who reach new people.

Another example is small groups. A church can experience tremendous growth by multiplying small groups. Again, what do you need to start small groups? You need a leader and you need new members. If you get the inside scoop on successful ministries, you will find they are built on developing leaders and reaching new people. Two examples in this generation are Rick Warren and Bill Hybels. Foundational staples of their ministries are the practices of developing leaders and reaching new people.

I have a friend who called the twenty-five fastest-growing churches in America and asked them if they had a written pathway for leadership development. What he found was crystal clear. Every single one of these ministries had a clear process—in writing—on how they went about developing leaders. An interesting note: These congregations had diverse types of senior leadership, they came from different denominations, they expounded various doctrines, and they approached the process of developing leaders differently. However, all of them were absolutely committed to learning how to consistently develop high-quality leaders in their organizations, and all of them were growing.

Multiply Leaders

It's time for honest questions: Does your church or ministry have a written leadership development pathway? Is your church or ministry consistently producing new high-quality leaders who are reaching new people? Think about it from a personal level. Have you developed other leaders who are reaching new people?

I have studied major Christian movements throughout history and what becomes obvious is wherever you see a leader focused on developing others and reaching new people, you see multiplication. This is historically true no matter the time, political climate, or geographical location. In history, wherever you see leaders who focus on developing someone close to them and reaching out to others, you find growth.

Take, for example, Elias Keech. He came to the New Americas, was converted under his own preaching, founded the oldest remaining church in America, and started reaching new people by establishing preaching points that became new congregations. Another notable example is Dan Taylor, who empowered resurgent growth in England by starting new connection groups and developing a training center for new leaders. Out of the Great Awakening revivals, led by Jonathan Edwards and George Whitfield, came New Light groups that raised up new leaders and reached many new people. Johann Oncken of Germany adopted the motto "Every Baptist a missionary." During a tremendous time of persecution (the state church killed and hung people in suspended cages from church spires), he started developing new leaders and pioneering small pietist home groups to reach new people. Regardless of the political, geographic, or denominational climate, church history is built on visionary leaders developing leaders and reaching new people.

How can we wield our influence to develop leaders and reach new people? I want to share with you three words that have been tremendously beneficial to me: Recruit, Coach, Repeat. In this session we are going to take disciple making to the next level as we focus on the skill of multiplying leaders who make disciples through recruiting, coaching, and repeating the process.

We will do this by employing the essential disciple-making skills we have already been utilizing: the Reach List, praying for and with others, showing people we care, sharing our stories, giving personal invitations, and gathering people into groups. Each one of these essential skills can be used to multiply leaders and inspire a whole lot of people to follow Jesus.

How It Works and Why It Matters

Recruit

Who's on your bench? Years ago I attended a national Christian leaders meeting in Chicago, Illinois. The venue was first-class. The music was inspirational. The hospitality of the host church was exceptional. I was totally impressed. At the end of the day, there was a special "invitation only" meeting where all the behind-the-scenes insights were shared. During this meeting, I expressed to the person next to me what a wonderful, high-quality experience this day had been.

As I was talking to my new friend, the next speaker had taken the podium and was beginning to share. There was nothing notably impressive about the speaker. I would use the word "ordinary" to describe him. His clothes were a bit disheveled and I had a hard time understanding what he was saying. He was neither dynamic nor engaging, and didn't speak very clearly at all. I was wondering to myself, *Who is this guy and why is he on stage?* When I asked my friend who the guy was, he said, "That is the pastor who grew this church from nothing to what it is today."

WOW!

I had to get to know this guy and find out his secret. How could a guy like that grow something like this? I was thoroughly impressed and intrigued. So I made a point to get some one-on-one time with him. I asked him what he thought contributed to his success. He said, basically, "Every leader needs people on his or her bench. Three deep on every leadership bench." It was his practice when he passed a leader in the congregation to ask them, "Tell me, who's on your bench?" He expected his leaders to be developing three other people all the time. He said that if after a number of inquiries, a leader continued to have no one on his/her bench, that person didn't stay in leadership position.

I learned two valuable lessons from an ordinary looking man who was an extraordinary leader. First, always have at least three people on my leadership development bench, and ensure that every leader in my ministry or organization has people on his or her bench. Second, you get what you inspect, not what you expect. I went home inspired to start building a ministry bench and to start inspecting the results. My only regret is, I wish I had started sooner. If you want to develop leaders and reach new people, start recruiting a bench and start inspecting results. Who's on your bench?

Start recruiting people today for your bench. Pull out your Reach List and start making a three-person Lead List. The goal is to get three deep on the bench. This list is your Peter, James, and John, with whom you will share mountaintop highs and valley lows together. A Lead List is a list of three people you are working to recruit to be on your leadership development bench.

Recruit them and begin to teach them how to discover and develop what we have covered in *Discipleship Uncomplicated*. Do not say NO for anyone! I have been surprised over and over again by the people who have given me the privilege of sharing the disciple-making journey with them. Multiplying leaders is a skill, and like the other skills it takes some work to develop, but you can do it and the results are well worth it.

Coach

Once we recruit leaders, we need to coach them to be successful. During coaching, focus on skill development. This is not general "You figure it out" coaching. Rather, this is specific skill-based coaching. We are coaching for specific disciple-making results. Here is a basic outline for coaching another person:

1. Begin the session with your focus on the person you are mentoring for success. Genuinely care about the other person or don't do it! Here's where to start: "Tell me how you are doing" or "Tell me how things are going." Tone of voice is important.

2. Coach the heart: "Tell me what are you learning about loving God and loving people" or "Have you faced any challenges lately?" or "Have you seen any good examples?"

3. Coach to develop each of the skills covered in *Discipleship Uncomplicated*. Do not quit until you have coached your mentees to successfully integrate these skills into everyday life.

4. Coach to reach new people by saying, "Tell me about someone you have recently added to your Reach List."

5. Coach to develop new leaders by saying, "Tell me about someone you would like to see on your Lead List or leadership bench."

"How are things going?" Begin each coaching session by taking a genuine interest in the people you are meeting with. Let them know they are important. Share some stories, listen to what is going on in their lives, laugh, share concern, and pray with each other. Let them know you appreciate their taking the time to meet with you. Share that you are excited about what God is doing. Celebrate any and all progress and seek to inspire them. This should be fun.

Coach the heart. Never forget that everything that is eternally important depends on loving God and loving people. Our love for God and our love for people will not grow without intentional focus and direction. Every time I ask the question "What are you learning about loving God and loving people?" I am reminded that this is what all the Law and the Prophets and eternal life are hanging on.

This is what brings meaning, purpose, and joy to everyday life. As I listen to what others are learning about loving God and loving people, I learn how I can better fulfill these two great commandments. The difference between leadership and manipulation is motive. Loving God and loving people are the greatest motives we can live by. As these two commandments take up residence in our lives, they become our flesh-and-blood gospel.

Coach successful skill integration. Here we coach through each of these skills and inspect the results until we lead others to integrate these skills into everyday life. A skill is something we have learned so well that we can use it when we need it. Skill integration is key to everyday disciple making. If we can't employ the skill in real time when opportunities are ripe, we haven't learned it. A skill is not something we learn and forget. A skill is something we learn and carry with us all our lives. Focus on skill integration. Each challenge moves us to engage people relationally, spiritually, and developmentally. Investing in others is the heart of disciple making.

As you inspire others to develop the skills covered in *Discipleship Uncomplicated*, you are giving them what they need to be successful in the work of making disciples. Listen to each other and share your personal insights and stories with each other. As a coach I have gleaned generous amounts of inspiration and insights from the people I have met with, and you will too.

Coaching requires that we give specific assignments, follow up, and celebrate every success. That is why each of these sections come with a challenge to complete. Coach your leaders through each and every challenge. Notice that each challenge carries three primary elements: *Reaching, Doing,* and *Teaching.* These specific assignments are where we start. For example, the first specific assignment given is to develop a Reach List and teach someone else how to develop a list. Jesus laid these elements out in the Great Commission. Reaching, doing, and teaching are foundational for making disciples.

Coach to reach new people. Using the section entitled "What's Your Name?" walk them through how God called people by name. Share one of the inspirational stories in the book, or share your own inspirational story. Guide them through the practical tips and get them started recording the first five names on their list. Do not leave until they have at least the first five names on their list. As soon as they begin to add names, I start celebrating their progress. Challenge and inspire them to complete the first challenge. Then set up your next get-together.

Adding people to the Reach List is an ongoing skill. It will be repeated in every challenge. Add at least one new person for every session you have. I personally set a goal to add one new person to my Reach List every week. The number of people on your list is not as important as the discipline of consistently adding people to your list. When we stop recruiting, we stop making disciples.

At the beginning of a meeting, I will share a story about a new name on my list, then I will ask them, "Now tell me about someone new on your list." A good friend of mine shared the M.A.W.L. method with me. Model, Assist, Watch, and Leave are wonderful guide stones to develop those on your bench. **M**odel what you want to multiply. **A**ssist where needed for them to experience success. **W**atch them so you can coach them up where needed. And **L**eave them when they can do it on their own.

Coach to develop new leaders. Recruiting is where we begin to multiply leaders and reach new people. I have learned there are many people, both in local congregations and in communities, who have a relationship with Jesus Christ, but have never been personally discipled. Right now there are many people who would readily spend time with you and allow you to sow these disciple-making skills into their lives. I have found that many people are waiting for a personal invitation to be a part of something that truly matters.

A positive interaction with a person you are recruiting employs the skills we have covered. We get to know them by name, pray for them, demonstrate that we care about them, listen to their stories/ share our stories, give them a personal invitation to go through *Discipleship Uncomplicated* with us, and gather them into a one-on-one or personal group.

As you start recruiting, here are a few suggestions. Start small and work out the bugs. I recommend starting by building a bench of three people. I simply follow the example of Jesus when he gathered Peter, James, and John. The pace of life is hectic for most people, and disciple making requires that we spend quantity personal time with them.

I have personally made many mistakes along the way, and recruiting more people than I could keep up with has been one of them. This cripples disciple-making momentum. If you find yourself canceling meetings or going weeks between them, then scale back the number of people you are investing in.

The goal is to multiply leaders who are reaching new people and multiplying their own leaders. When you embrace multiplying quality leaders, then being truly productive takes precedent over being busy. Busyness doesn't make us productive; results make us productive. Producing disciples who love and follow Jesus and inspiring others to do the same makes us productive disciple makers.

Start recruiting people from your Reach List and those the Lord brings into your life. Ask God to lead you and start extending personal invitations. You can recruit in person, over the phone, or by setting up a meeting.

Repeat

No multiplication has happened until the leaders on your bench have recruited, coached, and repeated the process of developing leaders. Repeating the process requires another layer of organization. Here is where we inspect the benches of our leaders. Do your leaders have a bench that is three deep? This is captured in #5 of the above coaching session. Develop new leaders by saying, "Tell me about someone you would like to see on your Lead List or leadership bench."

I used to think everything waited on being intentional. I have since learned that is simply not true. You can't be intentional about something you are not aware of. First, we have to *become aware* before we can become intentional. Everything waits on awareness! And yes, once we become aware of an opportunity, then we must *take action* to move into that God moment. This has been a long, painful journey as the Lord has had to pry my eyes open to the countless opportunities He has set before me and I have simply walked by.

I have learned that many people are just like me—unaware of the opportunities around them to make disciples. Sometimes we as leaders need to help people discover these opportunities. Sharing your God stories is a great way to create a greater awareness. Invite your leaders to go with you when you are recruiting someone to your bench. Nothing trumps personal experience as a teaching tool.

Multiplying leaders who are helping others to discover and develop these disciple-making skills keeps the repeat cycle going. No new leaders—no multiplication! The heart of disciple making is loving God and loving people. The bones of disciple making are developing leaders and reaching new people. The muscles and motor that move disciple making are these skills we have covered in *Discipleship Uncomplicated*. It's time to get those muscles in shape and start moving mountains. May the Lord Jesus Christ increase your awareness and influence, and you make it your business to make disciples who love God, love people, and make disciples.

The Practical: How to Multiply Leaders

TIP #1 Use your Reach List and fashion a Lead List with three names and best contact information. Get three deep on the bench.

1. _____#_____

2. _____#_____

3. _____#_____

TIP #2 Contact the first three people you want to see on your Lead List personally invite them to develop some disciple-making skills.

TIP #3 A great way to form the personal invitation is to say something like "I want you to develop some disciple-making skills with me, what do you say?" No Christian speed dating!

TIP #4 Go over the five-step coaching process.

1. Begin the session with your focus on the person you are there to help be successful. Genuinely care about the other

person or don't do it! Here's a way to start: "Tell me how you are doing" or "Tell me how things are going." Tone of voice is important.

2. Coach the heart: "Tell me, what are you learning about loving God and loving people?" "Have you faced any challenges lately?" or "Have you seen any good examples?"

3. Coach to develop each of the skills covered in *Discipleship Uncomplicated*. (Do not quit until you have coached them to successfully integrate each skill into everyday life.)

4. Coach to reach new people: "Tell me about someone you have recently added to your Reach List."

5. Coach to develop new leaders: "Tell me about someone you would like to see on your Lead List or leadership bench."

TIP #5 Secure copies of *Discipleship Uncomplicated* for those you will disciple.

TIP #6 Remember the M.A.W.L. method: Model what you want to multiply, assist where needed, watch to ensure success, and leave them to do it when they are able to do it well.

TIP #7 Recruit, Coach, Repeat

Therefore, go make disciples of people from all nations, baptizing them in the name of the Father, in the name of the Son, and in the name of the Holy Spirit. Teach them and show them how to live the commands I have entrusted to you. And I will always be with you. (Matthew 28:18-20)

Challenge

Ask one person "What's your name?" and write their name on your Reach List (remember to include where you met them). Next, personally invite three people to develop some disciple-making skills with you. Write their names:

1. _____

2. _____

3. _____

Finally, teach one person the importance of develop leaders and reaching people.

Start Guide

Would you like to know how to implement *Discipleship Uncomplicated* and start multiplying disciple makers in your ministry or congregation? Great! I have provided a step-by-step Start Guide to get you going.

The Four Steps

Step 1

Decide your start date _____.

Plan and promote three months out, and give yourself and your leaders time to personally recruit participants. Plan for nine sessions. A session can be once a month, once a week, or once every couple of weeks. Decide what works best for you.

Personally inspire and challenge your leaders to recruit three team members to go through *Discipleship Uncomplicated* with them. This is the first step to identifying who your leaders are. If a leader cannot recruit three people to make disciples, they are not a leader. Positions don't make a person a leader; the people who follow them make that person a leader.

Step 2

Decide on the number of teams you want to start with.

#_____ teams (x 4) = #_____ participants

For each team, you need a leader and three team members (1 team = 4 participants, 2 teams = 8 participants, etc.).

Step 3

Order a *Discipleship Uncomplicated* book for each of your disciple makers. Order them directly by emailing me at whhaynes@gmail.com to save money.

Step 4

Use this guidebook to lead your teams to discover and develop disciple-making skills.

Four and No More

We are about to embark on an incredible disciple-making journey together. Consider the time when Jesus invited Peter, James, and John to go with Him to the mountain. He wanted to share a personal and spiritually powerful experience with them.

Together on that mountain they came to know Jesus in a profound, life-changing way, and they heard God speak to them. This is the kind of journey we are embarking on. Together throughout this journey, we are going to come to know Jesus better and we are going to hear from God. Buckle up!

Using Jesus as our model, personally invite three people to come on this journey with you. Here is a sample of how I invite others:

"I would like you to go through something **with me**. It's called *Discipleship Uncomplicated*; we will learn skills that will help us in everyday life. These are skills Jesus used. Will you go through it **with me?**"

With me are the key words to giving personal invitations. Coach the people you lead to personally invite three people to form groups of four using the **"With Me"** approach. Personal invitations are much more productive than general announcements.

Who can we disciple? The only requirement for disciple making is finding someone willing to follow you. When Jesus wanted to make disciples, He said, "Follow Me." Jesus couldn't disciple someone who would not follow him and neither can we. If people will follow you, you can disciple them. Do not set up barriers and insist on requirements that Jesus didn't set up or insist on. Find three people who will follow you and get started.

Disciple Making Is a Team Sport

Consider Mark 2:1-12: Four friends find a way to get their friend to Jesus. This captures the essence of disciple making. These friends overcome all kinds of barriers, obstacles, and excuses. They worked together until they figured out how to get their friend in front of Jesus. We will form groups of four and forge friendships, develop new skills, overcome barriers, and work together until we get our friends in front of Jesus.

List of Team Members
(You and Three Others)

	Name	Best Contact
1.	_____ #	_____
2.	_____ #	_____
3.	_____ #	_____
4.	_____ #	_____

These teams will work together, stay together, and complete the *Discipleship Uncomplicated* together.

Upon completion, form NEW teams. This allows new friendships to develop. Friendships keep people connected and also keep people from leaving. If you are implementing this into small groups, Sunday school, or other groups, you MUST form groups of four to maximize effectiveness. List and track each team's progress. You get what you inspect, not what you expect.

DO NOT skip this.

Session 1

Love God, Love People

The Heartbeat of Disciple Making

Enthusiastic Welcome

Welcome to *Discipleship Uncomplicated*. I'm so glad you are here. We have a great experience planned for you. I want you to get in your teams or form groups of four.

Create a Team List with names and best contact information for your team.

	Name		Best Contact
1.		#	
2.		#	
3.		#	
4.		#	

Focus

Today we are going to look at the heartbeat of disciple making: loving God and loving people! Say this with me: Love God, love people! (RE-PEAT to get everyone involved.) The disciple-maker's heart beats with love for God and love for people. If we miss this, we miss everything. (Read 1 Corinthians 13 and ask, how important is love?)

Foundation

Have you ever overlooked the obvious? Share a story about a time you have overlooked something obvious.

Let's take a look at Matthew 22:34-40. (Read it.) Now let's take a quick quiz:

1. The Pharisee was an expert in the _____ (law). That is like being an expert in the Bible.
2. What is the first and greatest commandment? _____ (Love) GOD.
3. What is the second greatest commandment? _____ (Love) people.
4. How much of the Bible hangs or depends on these two commandments? _____ (All)

How much of the Bible hangs or depends on loving God and loving people?

Share and Celebrate

Share an inspiring story about loving God and loving people. Use a story from the book, one of your own, or one from a participant.

Celebrate the people involved in this journey with you. Let them know that you are proud of them. Never forget, you get what you celebrate!

Group Activity

Point out that loving God and loving people forms the foundation of disciple making. Each one of the skills that we will practice is built on loving God and loving people. Pair up in your team and share with each other.

1. Tell me one story about your life.
2. Tell me one thing that energizes you.
3. Tell me one thing that challenges you.

Encourage active listening: Take a genuine interest in each other's lives and let each person share without interruption.

Team Member Assignment

Read through principle two (What's Your Name?) and complete the challenge.

Team Leader Assignment

Pray for your team by name every day this week and contact them to let them know you are praying for them by name this week. This challenge can be completed face-to-face, with a text, call, card, letter, note, sticky note, scrap piece of paper, email, or through social media.

Session 2

What's Your Name?

Make Disciple Making Personal

Enthusiastic Welcome

I'm so glad you are here. We have a great experience planned for you. It's time to get in our teams of four. (Read Luke 19:1-9.) Point out that Jesus called Zacchaeus by name and He invited Himself over for dinner. This is our new disciple-making strategy.

Inspect Team Assignment

Check it off!

____ Team members completed reading assignment: principle two (What's Your Name?).

____ Team members have each other's contact information.

____ Leader prayed for each member by name every day this week.

Focus

In this session we will develop the essential skill of knowing people by name and creating a Reach List.

Foundation

What would you pay for a list of names and contact information of the people your organization is *guaranteed* most likely to influence for Christ?

You can't buy a list like this, but you can build one. By creating a Reach List, each person or group will begin to identify the people they are most likely to influence for Christ based on two principles: Proximity and Intention!

Principle #1: Proximity

We are most likely to influence the people we are closest to. (Eight out of ten people come into a group through the influence of a friend or family member.) This is the power of proximity.

Principle #2: Purpose

We are most likely to influence the people we are purposely trying to influence. Therefore, based on the principles of Proximity and Purpose, each group can build a list of names and contact information that clearly identifies the people they are most likely to influence for Christ.

Exchanging names is the first action we can take to apply the principle of Proximity. This one skill quickly moves us from everyone to someone—from the general to the personal. Meeting people and exchanging names and contact information is a skill we must develop if we are going to make disciples. Because let's face it, it is impossible to disciple someone we don't know and can't contact. As we develop this skill, we find that meeting new people is not only essential for disciple making but also a lot of fun.

Share and Celebrate

Share an inspiring story about someone on your Reach List and the importance of knowing someone by name. Use a story from the book, one of your own, or allow one of the disciple makers to share a story. You want to champion the importance of getting to know people by name and building a Reach List.

Celebrate the people involved in *Discipleship Uncomplicated*. Let them know that you are proud of them. Never forget, you get what you celebrate!

Group Activity

Pair up in your teams of four. Ask them to share the names of five people on their Reach List and a word about how they know them. If a team member doesn't have five names, the group should help them get five names and complete the activity.

Team Assignment

Read principle three (Let's Pray) and complete the challenge.

Leader Assignment

Pray for each team member by name, and ask your team members about someone new they have met this week that they could add to their Reach List. This challenge can be completed face-to-face, with a text, call, card, letter, note, sticky note, scrap piece of paper, email, or through social media.

Session 3

Let's Pray

Bring Spiritual Power to Your Relationships

Enthusiastic Welcome

I'm so glad you are here. We have a great experience planned for you. It's time to get in our teams of four. Share a story about someone you prayed with this week. (Read John 17.) What would it have been like to take part in the prayer meeting? Then pair and share one thing that stood out to you about Jesus' prayer in John 17.

Inspect Team Assignment

Check it off!

____ Team members completed reading assignment: principle three (Let's Pray).

____ Team members completed challenge.

____ Leader prayed for and contacted members.

Focus

In this session we will develop the skill of praying for and with people on your Reach List.

Foundation

Praying with those on our Reach List brings an awareness of God's presence and immediately moves our relationships from personal to spiritual.

Share and Celebrate

Share an inspiring story about praying with someone. Use a story from the book or one of your own, or allow a disciple maker to share their story. (You want to promote the importance praying for and with those on the Reach List.)

Group Activity

Model praying the three Ps with a volunteer. Have each team pair up and direct them to pray the three Ps for each other by name.

Here's an example:

"Father, I pray that you would PROTECT _____. I ask that you would PROVIDE for _____ and give (him/her) wisdom to make the many decisions that they need to make every day, and I ask that _____ would PERSONALLY come to know you better and love you more."

Team Assignment

Read principle four (This is for You) and complete the challenge.

Leader Assignment

Challenge your team to pray the three Ps with someone on their Reach List, either in person or in writing, and have them share the results with you. This challenge can be completed face-to-face, with a text, call, card, letter, note, sticky note, scrap piece of paper, email, or through social media.

This is for You

Create Relational Breakthroughs

Enthusiastic Welcome

I'm so glad you are here. We have a great experience planned for you. It's time to get in our teams and check off our assignments. But before we do, let me share a story. (Share about how you—or someone who gave you inspiration—made a positive difference in your life. Read Matthew 5:13-16.) Do you find it challenging to accept who Jesus says you are?

Inspect Team Assignment

Check it off!

___ Team members completed read assignment: principle four (This Is for You).

___ Team members completed challenge.

___ Leader challenged team members.

Focus

In this session we will begin to develop the disciple-making skill of showing the people on our Reach List that we care about them.

Foundation

Showing we care for the people on our list creates breakthrough moments in our relationships. The good we do in the lives of others becomes the salt and light so they can taste and see that Jesus is good. There are two rules for doing good in the lives of others. Rule #1: The good we do must benefit the person we are doing good for (no strings attached). When Jesus did good, it immediately benefited the person who received it. Rule #2: The good we do must honor God. So stay away from illegal, questionable, or inappropriate activities. What Jesus did brought honor to His Father.

Share and Celebrate

Ask a disciple maker to present to share a story about a time someone did something for them that made a positive impact on their life.

Group Activity

Pair up and share a story with each other about a time someone did an unexpected good in your life.

Team Assignment

Read principle five (Let Me Share a Story; Tell Me Your Story) and complete the challenge.

Leader Assignment

Challenge your team to do an unexpected good in the life of someone on their Reach List and report back to you. This challenge can be completed face-to-face, with a text, call, card, letter, note, sticky note, scrap piece of paper, email, or through social media.

Session 5

Let Me Share a Story; Tell Me Your Story

Share Stories to Build Connections

Enthusiastic Welcome

I'm so glad you are here. We have a great experience planned for you. It's time to get in our teams of four. As we do that, let me share a story with you. (Share God's story, your salvation story, a biblical story, or life story of your choosing. Read Acts 26:1-27.) Like water from a spring, the gospel naturally flows from your story.

Inspect Team Assignment

Check it off!

____ Team members completed reading assignment: principle five (Let Me Share a Story; Tell Me Your Story).

____ Team members completed challenge.

____ Leader challenged and heard back from team members.

Focus

In this session we will begin to develop the essential skill of sharing your stories and listening to the stories of people on your list.

Foundation

Sharing stories does three amazing things in our relationships with others. First, stories create room in the lives of others for us and our message, and it creates room in our lives for them. Every time we share stories, we carry a little of each other with us. Second, stories inspire action. Personal experience is the most powerful agent for effecting change. A well-told story is the second most powerful motivator we can use. A well-told story allows a person to vicariously experience an event with their mind and emotions without having personally been there. Third, sharing stories builds relational connections . . . like synapses firing to create clear passages in our brains or Mr. Miyagi from *The Karate Kid* building muscle memory. Sharing stories builds connections with those we share them with. The key phrase for sharing one of your stories is "Let me share a story." The key phrase to get others to share their story is "Tell me your story."

Optional Expansion

Since there are four types of stories, you could spend four sessions to prepare your team how to share each one.

Session 1: Challenge the team to share *God's Story* with one of the people on their Reach List.

Session 2: Challenge the team to share *your story* with one of the people on their Reach List.

Session 3: Challenge the team to share a *life story* with one of the people on their Reach List.

Session 4: Challenge the team to share a *Bible story* with one of the people on their Reach List.

Share and Celebrate

Share an encounter where you told one of your stories and saw God work through it. (Option: Ask someone to share a story about a time they heard a story from someone that encouraged their relationship with Jesus.) Promote the importance of sharing stories with those on our Reach List *and* listening to theirs.

Group Activity

Pair up in your teams and share your salvation story with each other. Tell how you personally came to love and follow Jesus.

Team Assignment

Read principle six (With Me) and complete the challenge.

Leader Assignment

Challenge your team to listen to the story of someone on their list and share their salvation story with someone on their list and report back to you. This challenge can be completed face-to-face, with a text, call, card, letter, note, sticky note, scrap piece of paper, email, or through social media.

OPTION: You can adjust this challenge to four sessions by sharing each story with a different person on your Reach List. Remember, integrating the skill of sharing your story with others is the goal, not getting through a session.

Session 6

With Me

How to Move People Spiritually

Enthusiastic Welcome

I'm so glad you are here. We have a great experience planned for you. It's time to get in our teams. Let me share a story with you. (Share a story about how someone gave you a personal invitation that helped you come to know Jesus better. Read Matthew 4:18-25.) Jesus gave personal invitations and empowered others to follow Him.

Inspect Team Assignment

Check it off!

___ Team members completed the reading assignment, principle six (With Me.)

___ Team members completed challenge.

___ Leader challenged team members.

Focus

In this session we will practice the disciple-making skill of giving personal invitations.

Foundation

This may be one of the most powerful skills we can develop. Learning to give personal invitations is how we move people spiritually from here to there. When Jesus wanted to move fishermen, doctors, and IRS workers to become followers, He gave them a personal invitation. Think about what Jesus literally said to them: "Follow me, and I will make you fishers of men" (Matthew 4:19 KJV). Notice that the primary invitation was to relationship. And through relationship with Himself, He would introduce them to a world they couldn't know without Him. An invitation is not personal because we say it. It is personal because it leads to a personal relationship with us, just as it leads to a personal relationship with Jesus. The key phrase to giving a personal invitation is "WITH ME!"

Here is how it works. Say you're making a general announcement inviting people to come to a workday at church. If you have given many of these, you already know the response is going to be limited. Why? Because the only thing people are considering is whether doing yard work at church is more important than everything else in their life. Now imagine you approach ten people personally and say, "Would you come to the workday at the church *with me*?" Now their primary consideration is their relationship with you and their secondary consideration is the workday. Relationship is what empowers the personal invitations we give. It is important to understand that our spiritual journey is a series of invitations and positive responses, and giving personal invitations is how we help people on their spiritual journey as well.

Share and Celebrate

Share an inspiring story about how a personal invitation helped you come to know Jesus better, love Him more, or walk with Him more closely. Promote how important it is to give personal invitations if we are going to help people follow Jesus.

Group Activity

Pair up in your teams and share a story about how someone gave you a personal invitation that helped your relationship with Jesus.

Team Assignment

Read principle seven (Gather People) and complete the challenge.

Leader Assignment

Challenge your team members to give one of these personal invitation to a person on their list and report back to you.

1. "(Their name) _____, I want you to come to church with me. What do you say?"
2. "(Their name) _____, I want you to have _____ (lunch, breakfast, dinner, coffee) with me. What do you say?"
3. "(Their name) _____, I want you to meet with me and a few friends. What do you say?"

This challenge can be completed face-to-face, with a text, call, card, letter, note, sticky note, scrap piece of paper, email, or through social media.

Gather People

Gather People to Influence People

Enthusiastic Welcome

I'm so glad you are here. We have a great experience planned for you. It's time to get in our teams of four. Let me share a story with you. (Share a story about a one-on-one, group of friends, social group, or large group gathering that has helped your relationship with Jesus. Read Matthew 9:35-10:5.) Jesus gathered disciples and gave them purpose.

Inspect Team Assignment

Check it off!

___ Team members completed the reading assignment, principle seven (Gather People).

___ Team members completed challenge.

___ Leader challenged and heard back from team members.

Focus

In this session we will begin to develop the essential skill of gathering people on our Reach Lists.

Foundation

Jesus gathered people into four different types of groups. First, He gathered people one-on-one, and these formed mentoring and coaching moments that left a profound impact on those He shared them with. Second, He gathered people into groups of four to share a personal and spiritual experience that forged lasting friendships and shared life-changing truth with them. Third, He gathered a group of twelve that he shared life with and fashioned a great learning environment. Fourth, He gathered people into large groups where people shared an inspiring and often unforgettable experience together. As people we will naturally gather in these groups. Because these are natural movements, we can develop the skills to use each of these groups for disciple making like Jesus did.

Optional Expansion

Since there are four types and sizes of groups to gather people in, you can expand this session into four more sessions.

Session 1: Challenge the team to gather people from their Reach List one-on-one to share a disciple-making coaching/mentoring experience.

Session 2: Challenge the team to gather people from their Reach List in a group of four to share a personal disciple-making experience.

Session 3: Challenge the team to gather people from their Reach List's into a small group to share a disciple-making learning experience.

Session 4: Challenge all the teams in your organization to gather people from their Reach Lists into a large group meeting to share an inspirational disciple-making experience together.

Share and Celebrate

Share an inspiring story about how gathering with a group of people helped your relationship with Jesus. Use a story from the book or one of your own, or allow participants to share their story. Promote the importance of gathering with people in groups either one-on-one, with friends, in a small group, or in a large group.

Group Activity

Pair up in your groups of four and share with each other a time you were invited to a one-on-one, group of friends, small group, or large group gathering that had a positive impact on your relationship with Jesus and others.

Team Assignment

Read principle nine (Multiply Leaders) and complete the challenge.

Leader Assignment

Challenge your team to personally invite a person on their list to come to a large group church experience with them and report back how it went. This challenge can be completed face-to-face, with a text, call, card, letter, note, sticky note, scrap piece of paper, email, or through social media.

Multiply Leaders
Empower Rapid Advance

Enthusiastic Welcome

I'm so glad you are here. We have a great experience planned for you. It's time to get in our teams. As we gather, let me share a story with you. (Share a story about how someone helped you see you were capable of more than you thought you were. Read Luke 8:1-8 and 2 Corinthians 9:6.) We reap at the rate that we sow.

Inspect Team Assignment

Check it off!

___ Team members completed the reading assignment, principle eight (Multiply Leaders).

___ Ask team members who completed challenge to share their Lead List.

___ Leader challenged team members.

Focus

In this session we will begin to develop the disciple-making skill of multiplying leaders.

Session 8   Multiply Leaders

Foundation

Using the example of Jesus' gathering of Peter, James, and John, we began this journey by recruiting three people to develop disciple-making skills with us using *Discipleship Uncomplicated.* Now the process comes full circle. We will use the relationships we have been cultivating with those on our Reach List and the skill of giving a personal "With Me" invitation to recruit new teams of disciple makers.

Over our time together, we have gotten to know each other in a personal and spiritual way. We have prayed for each other, listened to each other's stories, learned from each other's example, and grown closer to Jesus together. What an amazing journey God has for us.

Multiplying disciples is a sure way to forge lasting friendships and empower the rapid advance of loving God and loving people. The foundation of any growing organization, ministry, or church is built on developing leaders and reaching new people. Jesus multiplied leaders. He began by personally recruiting the Twelve, who were with Him as He went through all the neighborhoods and communities. They were with Him as He taught about God's kingdom. They were with Him as He shared the good news of forgiveness and redemption. And they were with Him as He ministered to the sick and hurting (Matthew 9:35-36).

These twelve men soon turned into seventy-two. Jesus appointed these seventy-two and sent them two by two ahead of Him into the surrounding communities to share good news and announce His coming. They went out together, worked together, and came back celebrating together (Luke 10:1-17). There are many examples in the Bible of leaders developing others and reaching new demographics. Developing leaders and reaching new people are foundational pillars to any effective ministry.

Share and Celebrate

Share a few inspiring stories about how you have seen people grow as disciple makers. Share a story about how someone helped you become more of a leader. Use a story from the book or one of your own, or allow participants to share their story. Promote the importance of using whatever influence we have to lead and inspire people to follow Jesus.

Group Activity

Pair up in your teams and share with each other who is on your Lead List and something about them.

Team Assignment

Come to the *Discipleship Uncomplicated* disciple-making celebration.

Leader Assignment

Send an encouraging note to each of your team members this week expressing how much you love and appreciate them. Challenge them to send an encouraging note to the people on their Lead List and report back. This can be accomplished face-to-face, with a text, call, card, letter, note, sticky note, scrap piece of paper, email, or through social media.

Celebration Time

Enjoying All God Has Done and
Cheering Each Other ON

Enthusiastic Welcome

I'm so glad you are here. We have a great experience planned for you.

Planning Time

Plan Some Fun

If it doesn't cause people to laugh or at least smile, it's not fun. Think games, videos, skits, jokes, or special prizes.

Plan to Share

Ask people to share some of their favorite experiences. What were some of the moments that have inspired you?

Plan to Appreciate

Ask each leader to share the reasons why they appreciate each person on their team.

Plan to Celebrate

Celebrate the contacts that have been made, the prayers that have been prayed, the good that has been done, the stories that have been shared, and the personal invitations that have been given. Tally the combined Reach Lists and celebrate those God has given you to influence.

Plan to Eat

Plan a meal, banquet, or dinner together to celebrate the work you have put in. Be proud of the progress you have made and the relationships you have made.

Set the start date for the next round of

Discipleship Uncomplicated

Month _____ Day _____ Time _____

(Recommendation: train new teams in the FALL and SPRING.)

Make disciple making a priority by putting it on your calendar every year! If disciple making is not on your calendar, it's not a priority.

Discipleship *Un*complicated

Summary of the 8 Principles

1. Love God, Love People
2. What's Your Name?
3. Let's Pray
4. This Is for You
5. Let Me Share a Story; Tell Me Your Story
6. Come with Me
7. Gather People
8. Multiply Leaders

Maximize Your Impact

Request a personal consultation with
Warren Haynes or schedule him as a featured
speaker for your disciple-making event.

Send your request via
WARRENtalks.com

About the Author

Warren Haynes is the national director of contextualized leadership development for Gateway Seminary. Warren leads an expansive network of leadership centers that focus on empowering Christians to reach for their full potential. He has a Doctor of Ministry degree and serves as a faculty member for Gateway Seminary. Warren's passion is to inspire people to expand their leadership capacity, make disciples, and sharpen their communication skills. He speaks to youth, college students, churches, pastors, and state and national Christian leaders. He brings a fun and refreshing approach to interacting and influencing people. His uncomplicated disciple-making approaches work in small rural towns, bustling metropolitan cities, and international settings. Warren is a husband, father, and follower of Jesus Christ.